lonely planet

TUSCANY

ROAD TRIPS

Duncan Garwood,
Virginia Maxwell,
Nicola Williams

HOW TO USE THIS BOOK

Reviews

In the Destinations section:

All reviews are ordered in our authors' preference, starting with their most preferred option. Additionally:

Sights are arranged in the geographic order that we suggest you visit them and, within this order, by author preference.

Eating and Sleeping reviews are ordered by price range (budget, midrange, top end) and, within these ranges, by author preference.

Map Legend

Routes
- Trip Route
- Trip Detour
- Linked Trip
- Walk Route
- Tollway
- Freeway
- Primary
- Secondary
- Tertiary
- Lane
- Unsealed Road
- Plaza/Mall
- Steps
- Tunnel
- Pedestrian Overpass
- Walk Track/Path

Boundaries
- International
- State/Province
- Cliff

Hydrography
- River/Creek
- Intermittent River
- Swamp/Mangrove
- Canal
- Water
- Dry/Salt/Intermittent Lake
- Glacier

Highway Markers
- A6 Autostrada
- SS231 State Highway
- SR203 Regional Highway
- SP3 Provincial Highway
- E74 Other Road

Trips
- 1 Trip Numbers
- 9 Trip Stop
- Walking tour
- Trip Detour

Population
- Capital (National)
- Capital (State/Province)
- City/Large Town
- Town/Village

Areas
- Beach
- Cemetery (Christian)
- Cemetery (Other)
- Park
- Forest
- Reservation
- Urban Area
- Sportsground

Transport
- Airport
- Cable Car/Funicular
- Metro station
- Parking
- Train/Railway
- Tram

Note: Not all symbols displayed above appear on the maps in this book

Symbols In This Book

- Top Tips
- Link Your Trips
- Tips from Locals
- Trip Detour
- History & Culture
- Family
- Food & Drink
- Outdoors
- Essential Photo
- Walking Tour
- Eating
- Sleeping

- Sights
- Beaches
- Activities
- Courses
- Tours
- Festivals & Events
- Sleeping
- Eating
- Drinking
- Entertainment
- Shopping
- Information & Transport

These symbols and abbreviations give vital information for each listing:

- Telephone number
- Opening hours
- Parking
- Nonsmoking
- Air-conditioning
- Internet access
- Wi-fi access
- Swimming pool
- Vegetarian selection
- English-language menu
- Family-friendly
- Pet-friendly
- Bus
- Ferry
- Tram
- Train

apt apartments
d double rooms
dm dorm beds
q quad rooms
r rooms
s single rooms
ste suites
tr triple rooms
tw twin rooms

CONTENTS

PLAN YOUR TRIP

ROAD TRIPS

DESTINATIONS

ROAD TRIP ESSENTIALS

Florence (p52) Diners on Piazza Santo Spirito

CHRISTIAN MUELLER/SHUTTERSTOCK ©

WELCOME TO TUSCANY

As Florence's Renaissance skyline fades into the background, the open road beckons. Motoring through Tuscany's voluptuous, wine-rich hills is one of Italy's great driving experiences – and one of the many on offer in this fascinating part of the country.

When people imagine classic Tuscan countryside, they usually conjure up images of central Tuscany. However, there's more to this popular region than rolling hills, sun-kissed vineyards and avenues of cypress trees. The real gems are the historic towns and cities, most of which are medieval and Renaissance time capsules magically transported to the modern day.

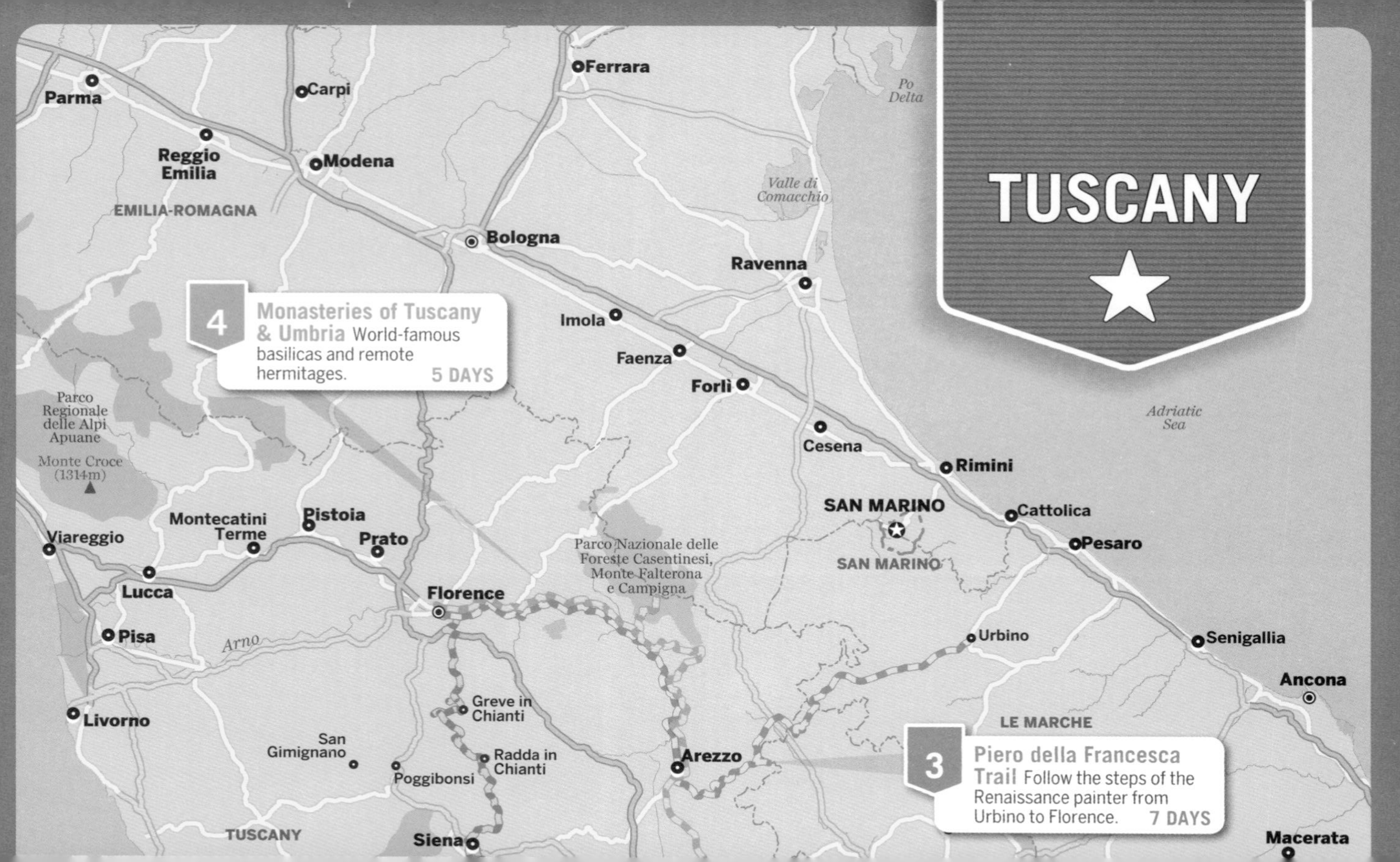
TUSCANY
4
Monasteries of Tuscany & Umbria World-famous basilicas and remote hermitages. 5 DAYS
3
Piero della Francesca Trail Follow the steps of the Renaissance painter from Urbino to Florence. 7 DAYS
Parma
Carpi
Ferrara
Reggio Emilia
Modena
EMILIA-ROMAGNA
Bologna
Valle di Comacchio
Po Delta
Ravenna
Imola
Faenza
Forlì
Cesena
Rimini
Adriatic Sea
SAN MARINO
SAN MARINO
Cattolica
Pesaro
Senigallia
Ancona
LE MARCHE
Macerata
Urbino
Parco Regionale delle Alpi Apuane
Monte Croce (1314m)
Viareggio
Montecatini Terme
Pistoia
Prato
Lucca
Florence
Pisa
Arno
Livorno
Parco Nazionale delle Foreste Casentinesi, Monte Falterona e Campigna
Greve in Chianti
Radda in Chianti
San Gimignano
Poggibonsi
Arezzo
Siena
TUSCANY

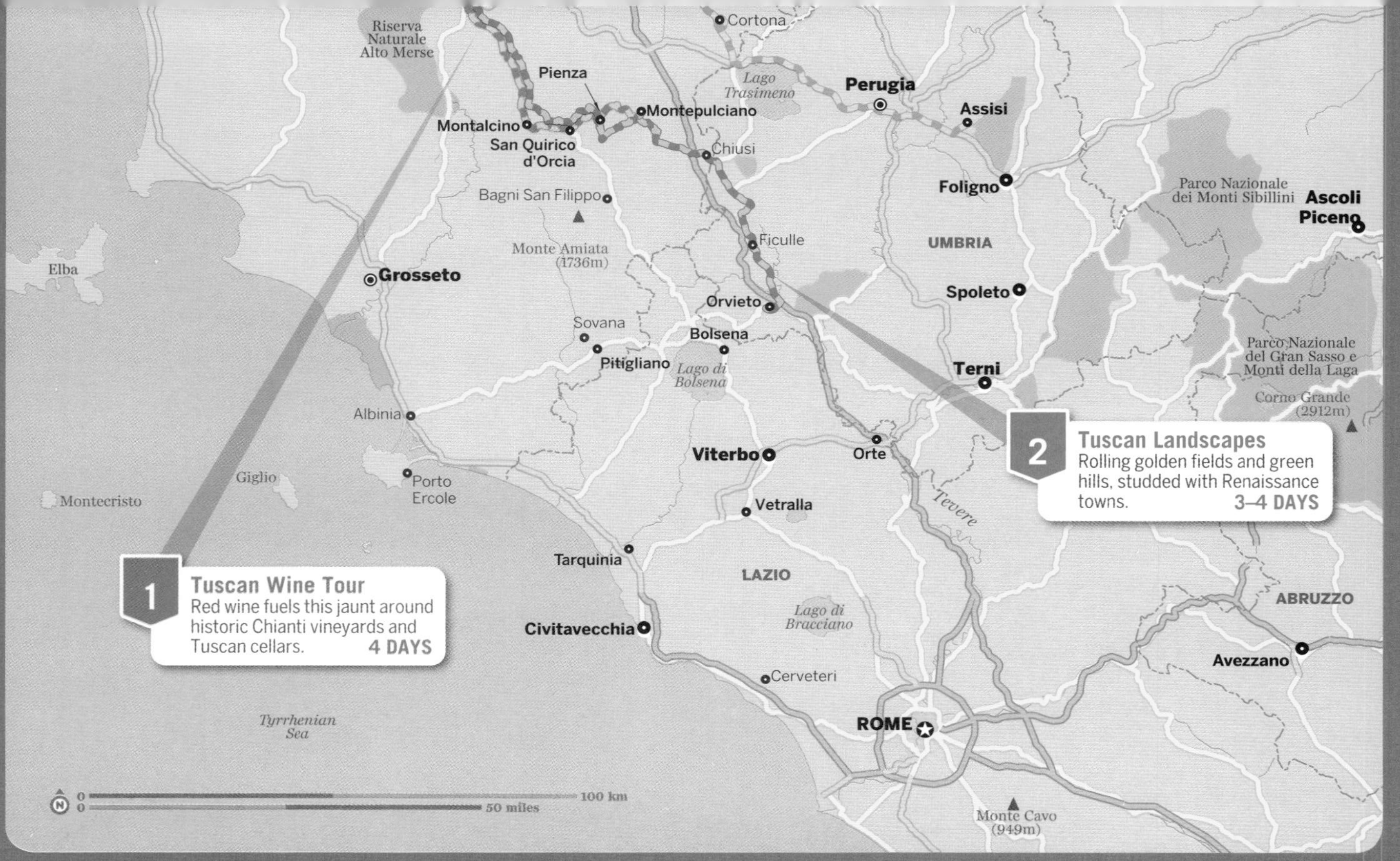

Tuscan Wine Tour
Red wine fuels this jaunt around historic Chianti vineyards and Tuscan cellars.
4 DAYS
Tuscan Landscapes
Rolling golden fields and green hills, studded with Renaissance towns.
3–4 DAYS
1
2
Riserva Naturale Alto Merse
Cortona
Pienza
Lago Trasimeno
Perugia
Assisi
Montalcino
Montepulciano
San Quirico d'Orcia
Chiusi
Foligno
Parco Nazionale dei Monti Sibillini
Ascoli Piceno
Bagni San Filippo
Ficulle
UMBRIA
Monte Amiata (1736m)
Elba
Grosseto
Spoleto
Orvieto
Sovana
Bolsena
Pitigliano
Lago di Bolsena
Terni
Parco Nazionale del Gran Sasso e Monti della Laga
Corno Grande (2912m)
Albinia
Viterbo
Orte
Giglio
Porto Ercole
Tevere
Montecristo
Vetralla
Tarquinia
LAZIO
ABRUZZO
Lago di Bracciano
Civitavecchia
Avezzano
Cerveteri
Tyrrhenian Sea
ROME
0
100 km
0
50 miles
Monte Cavo (949m)

HIGHLIGHTS

RASTISLAV SEDLAK SK/SHUTTERSTOCK ©

PHOTOCREO MICHAL BEDNAREK/SHUTTERSTOCK ©

Florence (above) With unrivalled architecture and exquisite arworks, Florence is magnetic, romantic and absorbing. See it on Trips 1 3 & 4

Val d'Orcia (left) Taste some of Italy's great wines and enjoy the provincial pace of some pretty towns. See it on Trips 1 & 2

Siena (right) An enchanting, beautifully preserved medieval city. See it on Trips 1 & 2

OLGYSHA/SHUTTERSTOCK ©

FLORENCE

Florence (Firenze) is one of the world's great art cities, with Renaissance icons and a wonderfully intact medieval centre. Beyond the Michelangelo masterpieces and Medici *palazzi* (mansions), there's a buzzing bar scene and great shopping in artisanal workshops and designer boutiques.

Getting Around

Nonresident traffic is banned from much of central Florence, and if you enter the Limited Traffic Zone (ZTL) you risk a fine of up to €200. Rather than drive, walk or use the city buses; tickets cost €1.50 or €2.50 on board.

Parking

There is free street parking around Piazzale Michelangelo and car parks (about €3.80 per hour) at Fortezza da Basso and Piazzale di Porta Romana. Otherwise, ask if your hotel can arrange parking.

Where to Eat

Florence teems with restaurants, trattorias, *osterie* (casual taverns) and wine bars catering to all budgets. Top neighbourhoods include hip Santa Croce, home to some of the city's best

DENNIS VAN DE WATER/SHUTTERSTOCK ©

restaurants, and the increasingly gentrified Oltrarno.

Where to Stay

To stay right in the heart of the action, the Duomo and Piazza della Signoria areas are a good bet with some excellent budget options. Near the train station, Santa Maria Novella has some good midrange boutique/design hotels.

Useful Websites

Firenze Turismo (www.firenzeturismo.it) The official tourist site is comprehensive and up-to-date.

Visit Florence (www.visitflorence.com) Practical advice and info on accommodation, sights and tours.

Firenze Musei (www.firenzemusei.it) Book tickets for the Uffizi and Accademia.

Trips Through Florence   

Destination coverage: p52

For more, check out our city and country guides. www.lonelyplanet.com

NEED TO KNOW

CURRENCY
Euro (€)

LANGUAGE
Italian

VISAS
Generally not required for stays of up to 90 days (or at all by EU nationals). Some nationalities will need a Schengen visa.

FUEL
Filling stations are widespread. Expect to pay around €1.46 per litre of unleaded petrol *(benzina senza piombo)*, €1.29 for diesel *(gasolio)*.

RENTAL CARS
Avis (www.avisautonoleggio.it)

Europcar (www.europcar.it)

Hertz (www.hertz.it)

Maggiore (www.maggiore.it)

IMPORTANT NUMBERS
Emergencies (Police ☎112, 113; Ambulance ☎115)

Roadside Assistance (☎80 31 16 from an Italian landline or mobile phone; ☎800 116800 from a foreign mobile phone)

Climate

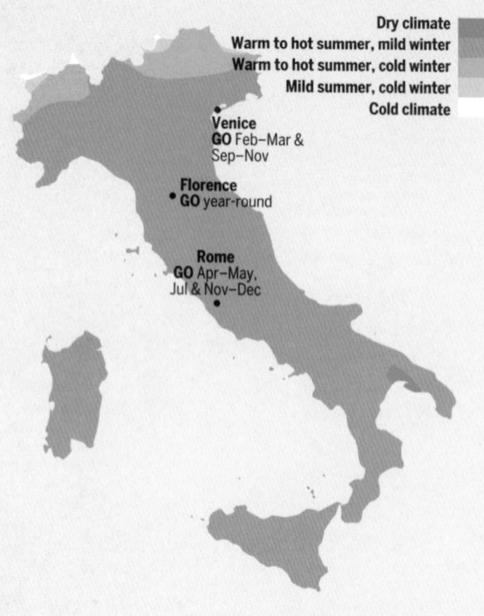

When to Go

High Season (Jul–Aug)
» Queues at big sights, and congested roads, especially in August.

» Prices also rocket for Christmas, New Year and Easter.

» Late December to March is high season in the Alps and Dolomites.

Shoulder (Apr–Jun & Sep–Oct)
» Good deals on accommodation, especially in the south.

» Spring is best for festivals, flowers and local produce.

» Autumn provides warm weather and the grape harvest.

Low Season (Nov–Mar)
» Prices up to 30% lower than in high season.

» Many sights and hotels closed in coastal and mountainous areas.

» A good period for cultural events in large cities.

Your Daily Budget

Budget: Less than €100

» Dorm bed: €20–35

» Double room in a budget hotel: €60–110

» Pizza or pasta: €6–15

Midrange: €100–250

» Double room in a hotel: €110–200

» Local restaurant dinner: €25–45

» Admission to museum: €4–18

Top End: More than €250

» Double room in a four- or five-star hotel: €200 plus

» Top restaurant dinner: €45–150

» Opera ticket: €40–210

Eating

Trattoria Informal, family-run restaurant cooking up traditional regional dishes.

Ristorante Formal dining, often with comprehensive wine lists and more sophisticated local or national fare.

Vegetarians Most places offer good vegetable starters and side dishes.

Price indicators for a two-course meal with a glass of house wine and *coperto* (cover charge):

€ less than €25

€€ €25–€45

€€€ more than €45

Sleeping

Hotels From luxury boutique palaces to modest family-run *pensioni* (small hotels).

B&Bs Rooms in restored farmhouses, city townhouses or seaside bungalows.

Agriturismi Farm stays range from working farms to luxury rural retreats.

Room Tax A nightly occupancy tax is charged on top of room rates.

Price indicators for a double room with private bathroom (breakfast included) in high season:

€ less than €110

€€ €110–€200

€€€ more than €200

Arriving in Tuscany

Pisa International Airport

Buses LAM Rossa (red) buses run into central Pisa (€1.20, 10 minutes).

Trains PisaMover automated trains run to Pisa's Stazione Pisa Centrale (€5, five minutes); regular trains run to/from Florence's Stazione di Santa Maria Novella (€8.70, 50 to 80 minutes).

Taxis Taxis cost €10 to central Pisa.

Florence Airport

Trams Trams run to/from Florence's Stazione di Santa Maria Novella (€1.50 from ticket machines at tram stops or €2.50 on board; 22 minutes).

Buses Volainbus shuttle buses (€6; 20 to 30 minutes) head to the central bus station.

Taxis Taxis cost a fixed €22 to central Florence (€24 on Sunday and holidays, €25.30 between 10pm and 6am), plus €1 per bag and €1 supplement for a fourth passenger.

Mobile Phones

Local SIM cards can be used in European, Australian and some unlocked US phones. Other phones must be set to roaming.

Internet Access

Free wi-fi is available in most hotels, hostels, B&Bs and *agriturismi* (farm stays), and in many bars and cafes.

Money

ATMs are widespread in Italy. Major credit cards are widely accepted, but some smaller shops, trattorias and hotels might not take them.

Tipping

Not obligatory but round up the bill or leave a euro or two in pizzerias and trattorias; 5% to 10% in smart restaurants.

Useful Websites

Lonely Planet (www.lonelyplanet.com/italy) Destination information, hotel bookings, traveller forum and more.

ENIT (www.italia.it) Official Italian-government tourism website.

For more, see Road Trip Essentials (p104).

Road Trips

Perugia (p94), Umbria
PAVEL068/SHUTTERSTOCK ©

Tuscan Wine Tour

Tuscany has its fair share of highlights, but few can match the indulgence of a drive through its wine country – an intoxicating blend of scenery, acclaimed restaurants and ruby-red wine.

TRIP HIGHLIGHTS

START
Florence

34 km
Greve in Chianti
Taste Tuscany's best at Greve's vast cellar

4
3
Panzano in Chianti

Radda in Chianti

Badia a Passignano
Idyllically located wine estate and medieval abbey

41 km

6

67 km
Castello di Ama
Enjoy modern art and excellent Chianti Classico

Siena

FINISH
Montepulciano

7

138 km
Montalcino
A fortified hill town, home of Brunello di Montalcino

4 DAYS
185KM / 115 MILES

GREAT FOR...

BEST TIME TO GO

Autumn for earthy hues and the grape harvest.

ESSENTIAL PHOTO

Val di Chiana and Val d'Orcia panoramas from Montepulciano's upper town.

BEST FOR GOURMETS

Tuscan *bistecca* (steak) in Panzano in Chianti.

1 Tuscan Wine Tour

Meandering through Tuscany's bucolic wine districts, this classic Chianti tour offers a taste of life in the slow lane. Once out of Florence (Firenze), you'll find yourself on quiet back roads driving through wooded hills and immaculate vineyards, stopping off at wine estates and hilltop towns to sample the local vintages. En route, you'll enjoy soul-stirring scenery, farmhouse food and some captivating towns.

1 Florence (p52)

Whet your appetite for the road ahead with a one-day cooking course at the **Cucina Lorenzo de' Medici** (334 3040551; www.cucinaldm.com; Piazza del Mercato Centrale, Mercato Centrale), one of Florence's many cookery schools. Once you're done at the stove, sneak out to visit the **Chiesa e Museo di Orsanmichele** (Via dell'Arte della Lana; church 10am-4.50pm daily, closed Mon Aug, museum 10am-4.50pm Mon, 10am-12.30pm Sat), an inspirational 14th-century church and one of Florence's lesser-known gems. Over the river, you can stock up on Tuscan wines and gourmet foods at **Obsequium** (055 21 68 49; www.obsequium.it; Borgo San Jacopo 17/39; 11am-9pm Mon-Sat, from noon Sun), a well-stocked wine shop on the ground floor of a medieval tower. Or, explore the old town on foot before you hit the road.

The Drive » From Florence it's about an hour to Verrazzano. Head south along the scenic SR222 (Via Chiantigiana) towards Greve. When you get to Greti, you'll see a shop selling wine from the Castello di Verrazzano and, just before it, a right turn up to the castle.

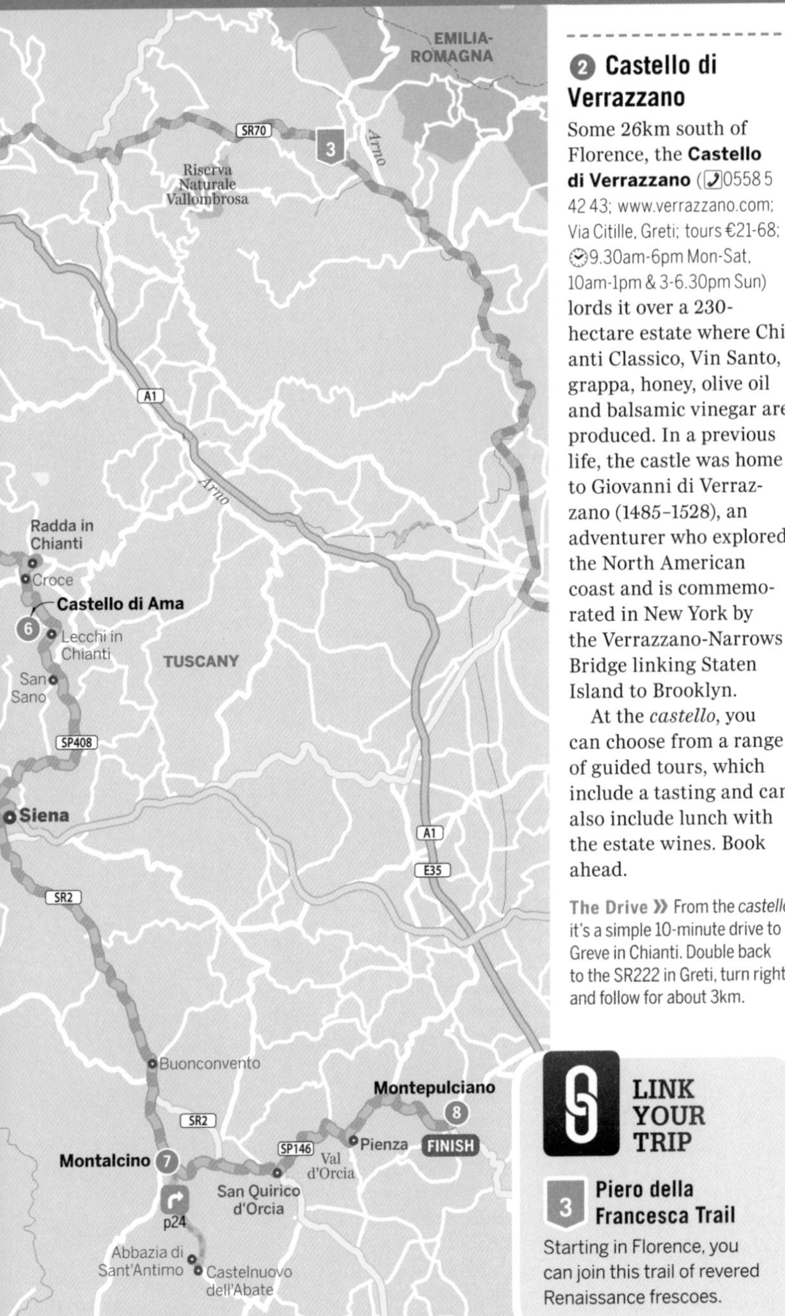

2 Castello di Verrazzano

Some 26km south of Florence, the **Castello di Verrazzano** (☎0558 5 42 43; www.verrazzano.com; Via Citille, Greti; tours €21-68; ⌚9.30am-6pm Mon-Sat, 10am-1pm & 3-6.30pm Sun) lords it over a 230-hectare estate where Chianti Classico, Vin Santo, grappa, honey, olive oil and balsamic vinegar are produced. In a previous life, the castle was home to Giovanni di Verrazzano (1485–1528), an adventurer who explored the North American coast and is commemorated in New York by the Verrazzano-Narrows Bridge linking Staten Island to Brooklyn.

At the *castello*, you can choose from a range of guided tours, which include a tasting and can also include lunch with the estate wines. Book ahead.

The Drive » From the *castello* it's a simple 10-minute drive to Greve in Chianti. Double back to the SR222 in Greti, turn right and follow for about 3km.

LINK YOUR TRIP

3 Piero della Francesca Trail

Starting in Florence, you can join this trail of revered Renaissance frescoes.

TUSCAN REDS

Something of a viticultural powerhouse, Tuscany excites wine buffs with its myriad full-bodied, highly respected reds. Like all Italian wines, these are classified according to strict guidelines, with the best designated *Denominazione di Origine Controllata e Garantita* (DOCG), followed by *Denominazione di Origine Controllata* (DOC) and *Indicazione di Geografica Tipica* (IGT).

Chianti

Cheery, full and dry, contemporary Chianti gets the thumbs up from wine critics. Produced in eight subzones from Sangiovese and a mix of other grape varieties, Chianti Classico is the best known, with its Gallo Nero (Black Cockerel) emblem, which once symbolised the medieval Chianti League. Young, fun Chianti Colli Senesi from the Siena hills is the largest subzone; Chianti delle Colline Pisane is light and soft in style; and Chianti Rùfina comes from the hills east of Florence.

Brunello di Montalcino

Brunello is among Italy's most prized wines. The product of Sangiovese grapes, it must be aged for a minimum of 24 months in oak barrels and four months in bottles, and cannot be released until five years after the vintage. Intense and complex with an ethereal fragrance, it is best paired with game, wild boar and roasts. Brunello grape rejects go into Rosso di Montalcino, Brunello's substantially cheaper but wholly drinkable kid sister.

Vino Nobile di Montepulciano

Prugnolo Gentile grapes (a clone of Sangiovese) form the backbone of the distinguished Vino Nobile di Montepulciano. Its intense but delicate nose and dry, vaguely tannic taste make it the perfect companion to red meat and mature cheese.

Super Tuscans

Developed in the 1970s, the Super Tuscans are wines that fall outside the traditional classification categories. As a result they are often made with a combination of local and imported grape varieties, such as merlot and cabernet. Sassacaia, Solaia, Bolgheri, Tignanello and Luce are all super-hot Super Tuscans.

TRIP HIGHLIGHT

3 Greve in Chianti (p80)

The main town in the Chianti Fiorentino, the northernmost of the two Chianti districts, Greve in Chianti has been an important wine centre for centuries. It has an amiable market-town air, and several eateries and *enoteche* (wine bars) that showcase the best Chianti food and drink. To stock up on picnic supplies, head to **Antica Macelleria Falorni** (☎0558 5 30 29; www.falorni.it; Piazza Giacomo Matteotti 71; ⏰9am-1pm & 3-7pm Mon-Sat, from 10am Sun), an atmospheric butcher's shop-cum-bistro that the Bencistà Falorni family have been running since the early 19th century and which specialises in delicious *finocchiona briciolona* (pork salami made with fennel seeds and Chianti wine). The family also run the Enoteca Falorni, the town's top cellar, where you can sample all sorts of local wine.

The Drive » From Greve turn off the main through road, Viale Giovanni di Verrazzano, near the Esso petrol station, and head up towards Montefioralle. Continue on as the road climbs past olive groves and through woods to Badia a Passignano, about 15 minutes away.

TRIP HIGHLIGHT

4 Badia a Passignano (p82)

Encircled by cypress trees and surrounded by swaths of olive groves and vineyards, the 11th-century **Chiesa di San Michele Arcangelo** (Abbey of Passignano; Via di Passignano; ⏲10am-noon & 3-5pm Mon-Wed, Fri & Sat, 3-5pm Sun) at Passignano sits at the heart of a historic wine estate run by the Antinoris, one of Tuscany's oldest and most prestigious winemaking families. The estate offers a range of guided tours, tastings and cookery courses. Most require prior booking, but you can just turn up at the estate's wine shop, **La Bottega** (☎0558 07 12 78; www.osteriadipassignano.com; Via di Passignano 33; ⏲10am-7.30pm Mon-Sat), to taste and buy Antinori wines and olive oil.

WINE TASTING GOES HIGH TECH

One of Tuscany's biggest cellars, the **Enoteca Falorni** (☎0558 54 64 04; www.enotecafalorni.it; Piazza delle Cantine 2-6; tastings by glass €0.60-30; ⏲10.30am-7.30pm Apr-May, to 8pm Jun-Sep, 10am-7pm Thu-Mon Oct-Mar, closed 3 weeks Jan) in Greve in Chianti stocks more than 1000 labels, of which around 100 are available for tasting. It's a lovely, brick-arched place, but wine tasting here is a very modern experience, thanks to a sophisticated wine-dispensing system that preserves wine in an open bottle for up to three weeks and allows tasters to serve themselves by the glass. Leave your credit card as a guarantee or buy a nonrefundable prepaid wine card (€5 to €100) to test your tipples of choice at the various 'tasting islands' dotted around the cellar. Curated tastings are also available.

The Drive » From Badia a Passignano, double back towards Greve and pick up the signposted SP118 for a pleasant 15-minute drive along the narrow tree-shaded road to Panzano.

5 Panzano in Chianti (p84)

The quiet medieval town of Panzano is an essential stop on any gourmet's tour of Tuscany. Here you can stock up on meaty picnic fare at **L'Antica Macelleria Cecchini** (☎0558 5 20 20; www.dariocecchini.com; Via XX Luglio 11; ⏲9am-4pm), a celebrated butcher's shop run by the poetry-spouting guru of Tuscan meat, Dario Cecchini. Alternatively, you can dine at one of his three eateries: the **Officina della Bistecca** (☎0558 5 20 20; Via XX Luglio 11; set menu adult/under 10yr €50/25; ⏲sittings at 1pm & 8pm), which serves a simple set menu based on *bistecca;* **Solociccia** (☎0558 5 27 27; Via XX Luglio; set meat menu adult/under 10yr €30/15; ⏲sittings at 1pm, 7pm, 8pm & 9pm), where guests share a communal table to sample meat dishes other than *bistecca;* and **Dario DOC** (☎0558 5 21 76; Via XX Luglio 11; burgers €10 or €15

TOP TIP: DRIVING IN CHIANTI

To cut down on driving stress, purchase a copy of *Le strade del Gallo Nero* (€2.50), a useful map that shows major and secondary roads and has a comprehensive list of wine estates. It's available at the tourist office in Greve and at **Casa Chianti Classico** (☎0577 73 81 87; www.chianticlassico.com; Monastery of Santa Maria al Prato, Circonvallazione Santa Maria 18; self-guided tour with glass of wine €7; ⏲tours & tastings 11am-7pm Tue-Sat, to 5pm Sun mid-Mar–Oct), the headquarters of the Consorzio di Chianti Classico in Radda.

PERSEOMED/GETTY IMAGES ©

CSP/SHUTTERSTOCK ©

WHY THIS IS A CLASSIC TRIP

DUNCAN GARWOOD, WRITER

The best Italian wine I've ever tasted was a Brunello di Montalcino. I bought it directly from a producer after a tasting in the Val d'Orcia and it was a revelation. It was just so thrilling to be drinking wine in the place it had been made. And it's this, combined with the inspiring scenery and magnificent food, that makes this tour of Tuscan wineries so uplifting.

Above: Wine cellar, Val d'Orcia
Left: Wine selection, Montalcino (p24)
Right: Stone house, Chianti

JANOKA82/GETTY IMAGES ©

Mon-Fri, €15 Sat, meat sushi €20; ⏲ noon-3pm Mon-Sat), a casual daytime eatery. Book ahead for the Officina and Solociccia.

The Drive » From Panzano, it's about 20km to the Castello di Ama. Strike south on the SR222 towards Radda in Chianti, enjoying views off to the right as you wend your way through the green countryside. At Croce, just beyond Radda, turn left and head towards Lecchi and San Sano. The Castello di Ama is signposted after a further 7km.

TRIP HIGHLIGHT

6 Castello di Ama

To indulge in some contemporary-art appreciation between wine tastings, make for **Castello di Ama** (☎0577 74 60 69; www.castellodiama.com; Località Ama; guided tours adult/under 16yr €15/free; ⏲ enoteca 10am-7pm, tours by appointment) near Lecchi. This highly regarded wine estate produces a fine Chianti Classico and has an original sculpture park showcasing 14 site-specific works by artists including Louise Bourgeois, Chen Zhen, Anish Kapoor, Kendell Geers and Daniel Buren. Book ahead.

The Drive » Reckon on about 1½ hours to Montalcino from the *castello*. Double back to the SP408 and head south to Lecchi and then on towards Siena. Skirt around the east of Siena and pick up the SR2 (Via Cassia) to Buonconvento and hilltop Montalcino, off to the right of the main road.

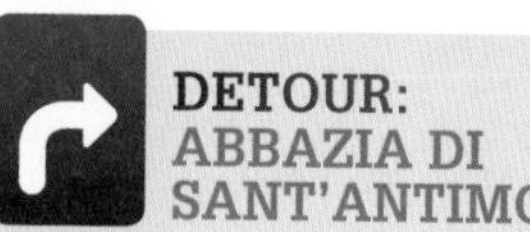

DETOUR: ABBAZIA DI SANT'ANTIMO

Start: 7 Montalcino

The striking Romanesque **Abbazia di Sant'Antimo** (☎0577 28 63 00; www.antimo.it; Castelnuovo dell'Abate; ⏲10am-7pm Apr-Oct, to 5pm Nov-Mar) lies in an isolated valley just below the village of Castelnuovo dell'Abate, 10.5km from Montalcino.

According to tradition, Charlemagne founded the original monastery in 781. The exterior, built in pale travertine stone, is simple but for the stone carvings, which include various fantastical animals. Inside, look for the polychrome 13th-century *Madonna and Child* and 12th-century *Crucifixion* above the main altar. The abbey's church, crypt, upper loggia, chapel, pharmacy and garden can be visited with a rented video guide (€6).

TRIP HIGHLIGHT

7 Montalcino (p84)

Montalcino, a pretty medieval town perched above the Val d'Orcia, is home to one of Italy's great wines, Brunello di Montalcino (and the more modest, but still very palatable, Rosso di Montalcino). There are plenty of *enoteche* where you can taste and buy, including one in the **Fortezza** (☎0577 84 92 11; Piazzale Fortezza; courtyard free, ramparts adult/reduced €4/2; ⏲9am-8pm Apr-Oct, 10am-6pm Nov-Mar), the 14th-century fortress that dominates the town's skyline.

For a historical insight into the town's winemaking past, head to the **Museo della Comunità di Montalcino e del Brunello** (☎0577 84 61 04; www.fattoriadeibarbi.it/museo-del-brunello; Fattoria dei Barbi, Località Podernovi 170; adult/reduced €5/2.50; ⏲10am-12.30pm & 2.30-6pm Thu-Tue Easter-late Nov), a small museum at the Fattoria dei Barbi wine estate, one of the oldest in the region.

The Drive » From Montalcino, head downhill and then, after about 8km, turn onto the SR2. At San Quirico d'Orcia pick up the SP146, a fabulously scenic road that weaves along the Val d'Orcia through rolling green hills, past the pretty town of Pienza, to Montepulciano. Allow about an hour.

8 Montepulciano (p87)

Set atop a narrow ridge of volcanic rock, the Renaissance centre of Montepulciano produces the celebrated red wine Vino Nobile. To sample it, head up the main street, called in stages Via di Gracciano nel Corso, Via di Voltaia del Corso and Via dell'Opio nel Corso, to the **Enoliteca Consortile** (www.enolitecavinonobile.it; Fortezza di Montepulciano, Via San Donato 21; ⏲2-6pm Mon, Wed & Thu, 11am-6pm Fri, 10.30am-7pm Sat & Sun), a modern tasting room operated by local wine producers. Housed on the ground floor of the town's Medicean fortress, it offers over 70 wines for tasting and purchase.

Chianti Greve in Chianti

ANDREA COMI/GETTY IMAGES ©

FRANCESCO RICCARDO IACOMINO/GETTY IMAGES ©

Tuscan Landscapes

Rolling hills capped by medieval towns, golden wheat fields and snaking lines of cypress trees – immerse yourself in Tuscan scenery on this trip through the region's southern stretches.

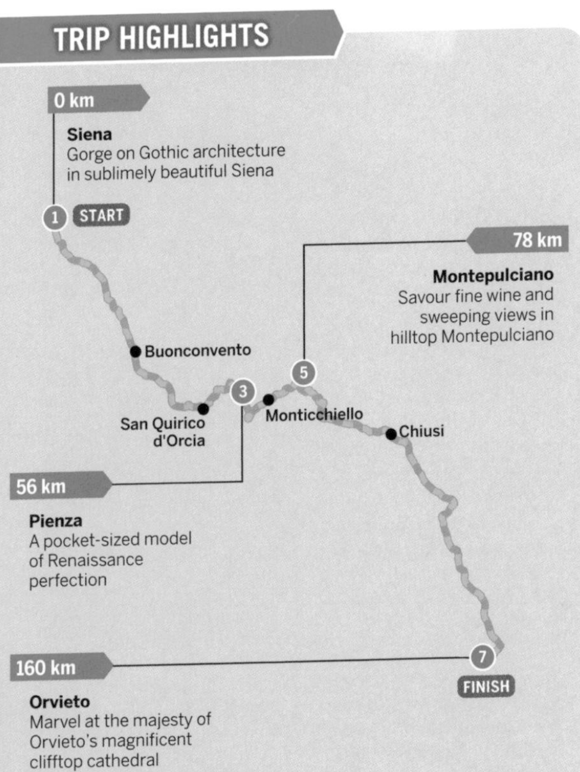

3–4 DAYS
160KM / 99 MILES

GREAT FOR...

BEST TIME TO GO

May to September for blue skies and fab photos.

ESSENTIAL PHOTO

The Val d'Orcia between San Quirico d'Orcia and Pienza.

BEST FOR RENAISSANCE ARCHITECTURE

Montepulciano's historic centre.

2 Tuscan Landscapes

Ever since medieval pilgrims discovered Tuscany en route from Canterbury to Rome, the region has been captivating travellers. This trip strikes south from Siena, running through the Crete Senesi, an area of clay hills scored by deep ravines, to the Unesco-listed Val d'Orcia, whose soothing hills and billowing plains are punctuated by delightful Renaissance towns. The end of the road is Orvieto, home to one of Italy's most feted Gothic cathedrals.

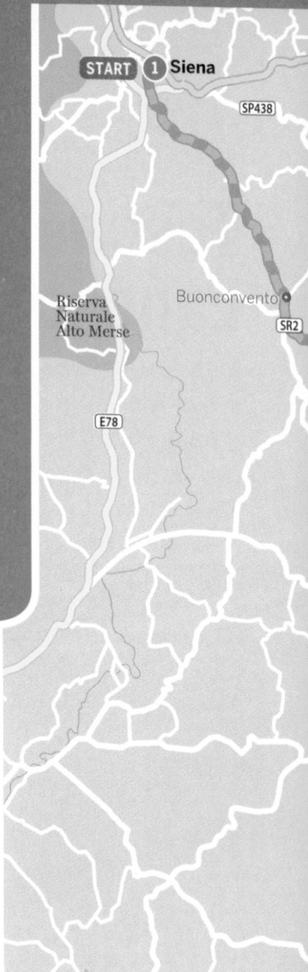

TRIP HIGHLIGHT

1 Siena (p74)

With its medieval *palazzi* (mansions) and humbling Gothic architecture, Siena's historic centre is a sight to compare with any in Tuscany. To admire it from above, climb to the top of the **Torre del Mangia** (☎0577 29 26 15; ticket@comune.siena.it; Palazzo Pubblico, Piazza del Campo 1; adult/family €10/25; ⏲10am-6.15pm Mar–mid-Oct, to 3.15pm mid-Oct–Feb), the slender 14th-century tower that rises above **Piazza del Campo**, and look down on a sea of red-tiled roofs and, beyond, to the green, undulating countryside that awaits you on this trip.

At the foot of the tower, **Palazzo Pubblico** (Palazzo Comunale; Piazza del Campo) is a magnificent example of Sienese Gothic architecture and home to the city's best art museum, the **Museo Civico** (Civic Museum; ☎0577 29 26 15; Palazzo Pubblico, Piazza del Campo 1; adult/reduced €10/9, with Torre del Mangia €15, with Torre del Mangia & Complesso Museale di Santa Maria della Scala €20; ⏲10am-6.15pm mid-Mar–Oct, to 5.15pm Nov–mid-Mar).

To the southwest of Palazzo Pubblico, another inspiring spectacle awaits. Siena's 13th-century **duomo** (Cattedrale di Santa Maria Assunta; ☎0577 28 63 00; www.operaduomo.siena.it; Piazza Duomo; Mar-Oct €5, Nov-Feb free, when floor displayed €8; ⏲10.30am-6.30pm Mon-Sat & 1.30-5.30pm Sun Mar-Oct, 10.30am-5pm Mon-Sat & 1.30-5pm Sun Nov-Feb) is one of Italy's greatest Gothic churches, and its magnificent facade of white, green and red polychrome marble is one you'll remember long after you've left town.

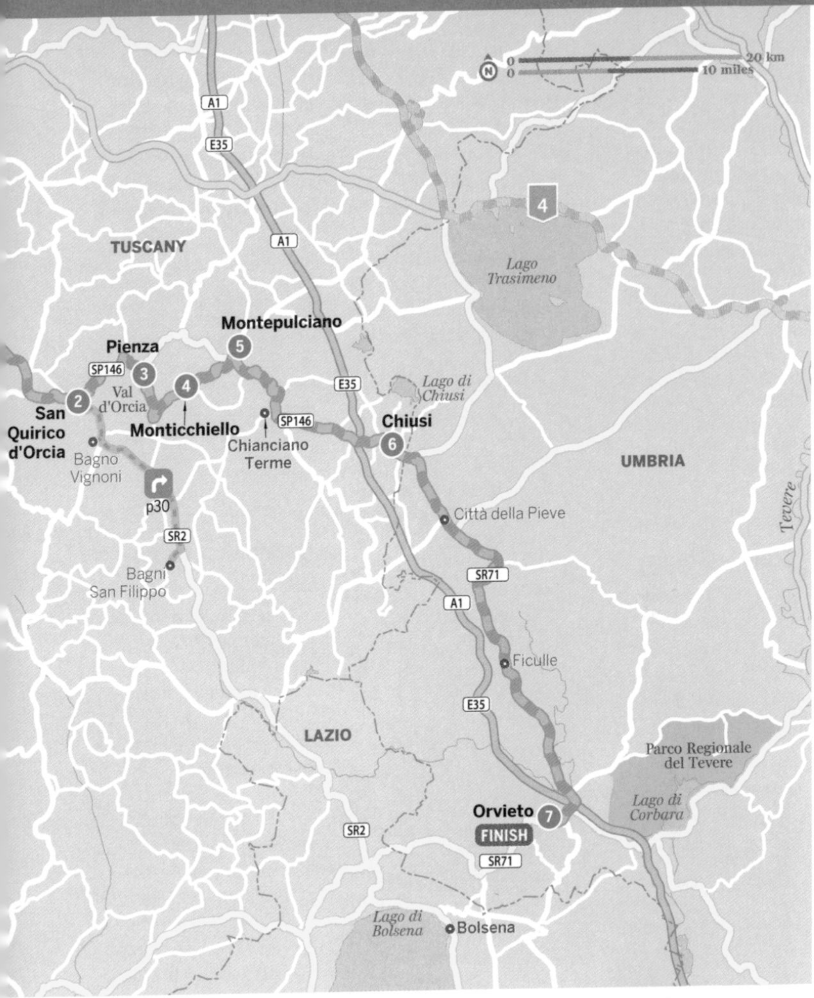

The Drive » The first leg down to San Quirico d'Orcia, about an hour's drive, takes you down the scenic SR2 via the market town of Buonconvento. En route you'll pass cultivated fields and swaths of curvaceous green plains.

2 San Quirico d'Orcia

First stop in the Unesco-protected Val d'Orcia is San Quirico d'Orcia. A fortified medieval town and one-time stopover on the Via Francigena pilgrim route between Canterbury and Rome,

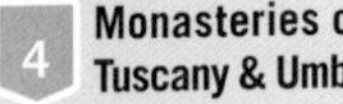

Monasteries of Tuscany & Umbria

Head east from Montepulciano along the SP438 to visit a string of ancient, isolated monasteries.

it's now a lovely, low-key village. There are no great must-see sights, but it's a pleasant place for a stroll, with a graceful Romanesque **Collegiata** (church) and formal Renaissance gardens known as the **Horti Leononi**.

The Drive » From San Quirico d'Orcia it's a quick 15-minute drive to Pienza along the SP146. This is one of the trip's most beautiful stretches, offering unfettered views over seas of undulating grasslands peppered by stone farmhouses and lines of elegant cypress trees.

TRIP HIGHLIGHT

3 Pienza (p86)

One of the most popular tourist destinations in the Val d'Orcia, pint-sized Pienza has a Renaissance centre that has changed little since local boy Pope Pius II had it built between 1459 and 1462. Action is centred on Piazza Pio II, where the solemn **duomo** (Concattedrale di Santa Maria Assunta; Piazza Pio II; ⏰7.30am-1pm & 2-7pm) is flanked by two Renaissance *palazzi* – on the right, **Palazzo Piccolomini** (☎0577 28 63 00; www.palazzopiccolomini pienza.it; Piazza Pio II; adult/reduced with guided tour €7/5; ⏰10am-6pm Tue-Sun mid-Mar–mid-Oct, to 4pm mid-Oct–mid-Mar, closed mid-Jan–mid-Feb & 2nd half Nov), the former papal residence; on the left, Palazzo Vescovile, home to the **Museo Diocesano** (☎0578 74 99 05; www.palazzoborgia.it; Corso il Rossellino 30; adult/reduced €4.50/3; ⏰10.30am-1.30pm & 2.30-6pm Wed-Mon mid-Mar–Oct, 10am-1pm & 2-5pm Sat & Sun Nov–mid-Mar) and an intriguing miscellany of artworks, manuscripts, tapestries and miniatures. Before leaving town make sure you pick up some of the local *pecorino* cheese for which the area is justly famous.

The Drive » From Pienza strike south on the SP18 and head into the heart of the countryside, enjoying more bucolic scenery as you go. After 6km or so you'll see a sign to Monticchiello off to the left. Take this road and continue for another 4km.

4 Monticchiello (p87)

A 15-minute drive southeast from Pienza brings you to Monticchiello, a sleepy medieval hilltop village with two good eateries. Choose between **Osteria La Porta** (☎0578 75 51 63; www.osterialaporta.it; Via del Piano 1; meals €45; ⏰9am-midnight), just inside the main gate, which has a small terrace with panoramic views of the Val d'Orcia; and stylish **Ristorante Daria** (☎0578 75 51 70; www.ristorantedaria.it; Via San Luigi 3; €40; ⏰12.15-2.30pm & 7.15-10pm Thu-Tue), a short walk away, which offers a menu of dishes that successfully marry rustic inspiration and refined execution.

The Drive » Take the SP88 and follow it as it ploughs on through fields and light woodland to the main SP146. Go

DETOUR: BAGNO VIGNONI & BAGNI SAN FILIPPO

Start: 2 San Quirico d'Orcia

Some 9km south of San Quirico d'Orcia along the SP53, hot sulphurous water (around 49°C) bubbles up into a picturesque pool in the centre of **Bagno Vignoni**. You can't actually enter the pool, but there are various spa complexes offering a full range of treatments. For free hot-water frolics continue 18km further along the SR2 to the tiny village of **Bagni San Filippo**, where there are thermal cascades in an open-air reserve. You'll find these just uphill from Hotel le Terme – follow a sign marked 'Fosso Bianco' down a lane for about 150m and you'll come to a series of mini pools, fed by hot, tumbling cascades of water. Not unlike a free, alfresco spa, it's a pleasant if slightly whiffy spot for a picnic.

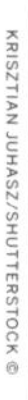

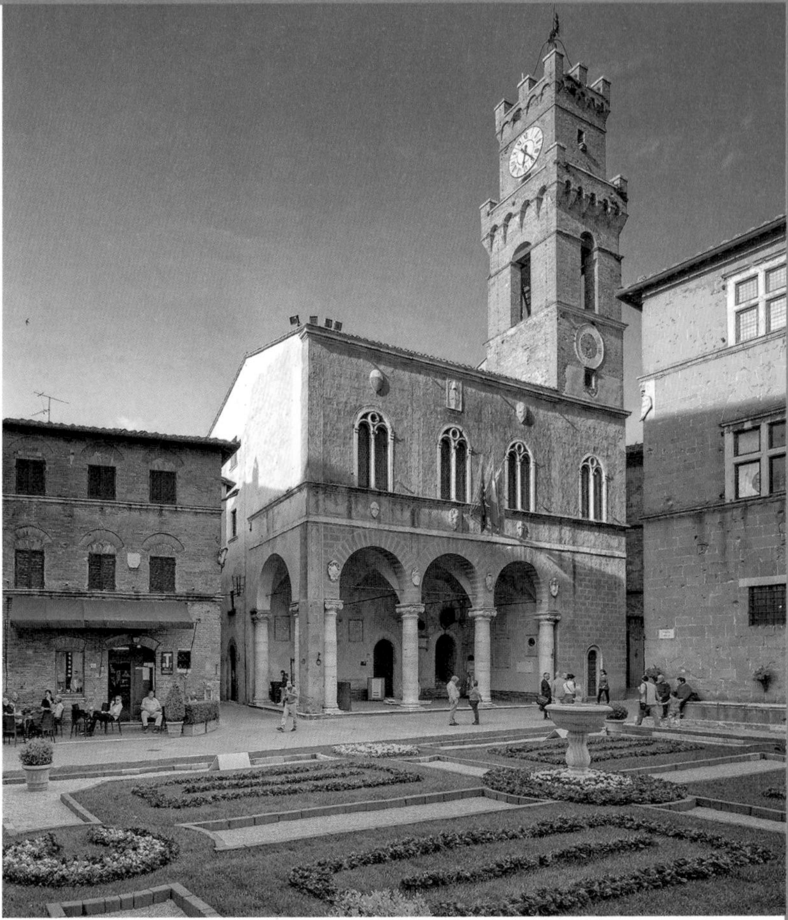

KRISZTIAN JUHASZ/SHUTTERSTOCK ©

Pienza Piazza Pio II

left and continue past orderly vineyards and olive groves up to San Biagio and 2km further on to Montepulciano. All told it takes about 20 minutes.

TRIP HIGHLIGHT

5 Montepulciano (p87)

Famous for its Vino Nobile wine, Montepulciano is a steeply stacked hill town harbouring a wealth of *palazzi* and fine buildings, as well as grandstand views over the Val di Chiana and Val d'Orcia. The main street, aka the Corso, climbs steeply, passing **Caffè Poliziano** (☎0578 75 86 15; www.caffepoliziano.it; Via di Voltaia 27; ⏰7am-9pm Mon-Fri, to 10.30pm Sat, to 9pm Sun; 📶), which has been operating since 1868, as it leads to the **Cantine Contucci** (☎0578 75 70 06; www.contucci.it; Via del Teatro 1; ⏰10am-12.30pm & 2.30-6pm), one of a number of historic wine cellars in town. Nearby **Piazza Grande** is flanked by the 14th-century **Palazzo Comunale** (terrace & tower adult/reduced €5/2.50, terrace only €2.50; ⏲10am-6pm Apr-Christmas) and the late-16th-century **duomo** (Cattedrale di Santa Maria Assunta; www.montepulcianochiusipienza.it; ⏲8am-7pm).

The Drive » Reckon on about 40 minutes to cover the 25km to Chiusi. From Montepulciano head southeast along the SP146 to Chianciano Terme, a popular spa town. Continue on towards the A1 autostrada, and Chiusi is just on the other side of the highway.

6 Chiusi

Once an important Etruscan centre, Chiusi is now a sleepy country town. Its main attractions are the Etruscan tombs dotted around the surrounding countryside, two of which are included in the ticket price of the impressive **Museo Archeologico Etrusco di Chiusi** (☎0578 2 01 77; www.facebook.com/museoetrusco.dichiusi; Via Porsenna 93; adult/reduced €6/3; ⏲9am-8pm) in the town centre. The museum has a bevy of ceramics, pottery, jewellery and cinerary urns dating from between the 9th and 2nd centuries BC.

The Drive » You have two choices for Orvieto. The quick route is on the A1 autostrada (about 45 minutes), but it's a more interesting drive along the SR71 (1½ hours). This passes through Città della Pieve, birthplace of the painter Perugino, and Ficulle, known since Roman times for its artisans.

TRIP HIGHLIGHT

7 Orvieto (p99)

Over the regional border in Umbria, the precariously perched town of Orvieto has one of Italy's finest Gothic cathedrals. The **Duomo di Orvieto** (☎0763 34 24 77; www.opsm.it; Piazza Duomo 26; €4, incl Museo dell'Opera del Duomo di Orvieto €5; ⏲9.30am-7pm Mon-Sat, 1-5.30pm Sun summer, shorter hours winter) took 30 years to plan and three centuries to complete. Work began in 1290, originally to a Romanesque design, but as construction proceeded, Gothic features were incorporated into the structure. Highlights include the richly coloured facade, and, in the **Cappella di San Brizio**, Luca Signorelli's fresco cycle *The Last Judgement*.

Across the piazza from the cathedral, the **Museo Claudio Faina e Civico** (☎0763 34 15 11; www.museofaina.it; Piazza Duomo 29; adult/reduced €4.50/3; ⏲9.30am-6pm summer, 10am-5pm winter, closed Mon Nov-Feb) houses an important collection of Etruscan archaeological artefacts.

Siena (p28) Torre del Mangia

CANADASTOCK/SHUTTERSTOCK ©

Piero della Francesca Trail

Follow in the footsteps of the Renaissance painter Piero della Francesca as you wind your way from medieval Urbino to Florence, stopping en route to admire his greatest works.

TRIP HIGHLIGHTS

0 km
Urbino
A charming Renaissance hill town surrounded by green peaks

67 km
Sansepolcro
Piero della Francesca's birthplace, a real hidden gem

110 km
Arezzo
Revel in sublime frescoes in the art-rich historic centre

185 km
Florence
Home to the world's greatest collection of Renaissance art

FINISH 6 · Passo della Consuma · Poppi · 5 · Monterchi · 3 · Passo di Bocca Trabaria · START 1

7 DAYS 185KM / 115 MILES

GREAT FOR...

BEST TIME TO GO

June to September for summer pageantry.

ESSENTIAL PHOTO

Views from the Passo della Consuma.

BEST FOR FILM BUFFS

Arezzo's Piazza Grande, a location for scenes in *La vita è bella* (Life is Beautiful).

Florence Galleria degli Uffizi (p40)

3 Piero della Francesca Trail

The Piero della Francesca trail was first advocated by the British author Aldous Huxley in *The Best Picture,* a 1925 essay he wrote in praise of della Francesca's *Resurrezione* (Resurrection). The roads have improved since Huxley's day but the trail remains a labour of love for art fans – it leads through dramatic Apennine scenery, over mountain passes and on to bustling medieval towns, culminating in Italy's revered Renaissance time capsule, Florence (Firenze).

TRIP HIGHLIGHT

1 Urbino

Hidden away in hilly Le Marche, the charming town of Urbino was a key player in the Renaissance art world. Its ruler, the Duca Federico da Montefeltro, was a major patron and many of the top artists and intellectuals of the day spent time here at his behest. Piero della Francesca arrived in 1469 and, along with a crack team of artists and architects, worked

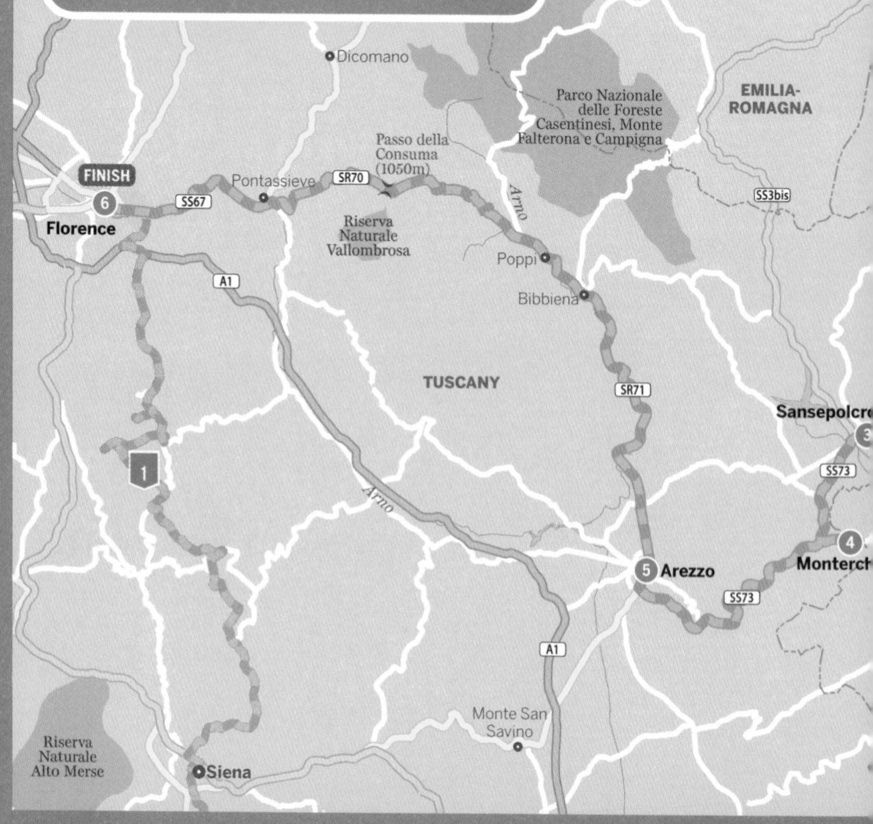

on the duke's palatial residence, the Palazzo Ducale. This magnificent palace now houses the **Galleria Nazionale delle Marche** (☎0722 32 26 25; www.gallerianazionalemarche.it; Piazza Duca Federico; adult/reduced €8/5; ⏰8.30am-7.15pm Tue-Sun, to 2pm Mon) and its rich collection of Renaissance paintings, including della Francesca's great *Flagellazione di Cristo* (Flagellation of Christ).

A short walk away, you can pay homage to Urbino's greatest son at the **Casa Natale di Raffaello** (☎0722 32 01 05; www.casaraffaello.com; Via Raffaello 57; €3.50; ⏰9am-1pm & 3-7pm Mon-Sat, 10am-1pm & 3-6pm Sun Mar-Oct, 9am-2pm Mon-Sat, 10am-1pm Sun Nov-Feb), the house where superstar painter Raphael was born in 1483.

The Drive » The 50km (one hour) drive up to the Passo di Bocca Trabaria involves hundreds of hairpin bends and tortuous climbing as it traverses a magnificent swath of Apennine mountains. From Urbino pick up the SS73bis and head through Montesoffio and Urbania before climbing up to the pass.

2 Passo di Bocca Trabaria

The Bocca Trabaria mountain pass (1049m) divides the Valtiberina (Tiber Valley), on the Urbino side, from the upper Valle del Metauro (Metauro Valley). It's a spectacular spot, well worth a quick pause, with sweeping views over the Apennines and several hiking trails heading into the surrounding mountains.

The Drive » Allow about half an hour for the 20km descent from Bocca Trabaria to Sansepolcro. For the first 15km or so the winding road plunges down the valley slopes to San Giustino, from where it's an easy hop northwest to Sansepolcro.

TRIP HIGHLIGHT

3 Sansepolcro (p72)

Birthplace of Piero della Francesca and home to two of his greatest works, Sansepolcro is an authentic hidden gem.

LINK YOUR TRIP

1 Tuscan Wine Tour

From Florence head south on the SR222 to the Castello di Verrazzano, one of the historic Chianti vineyards on this classic wine tour.

Its unspoiled historic centre is littered with *palazzi* (mansions) and churches harbouring great works of art, including the 14th-century **Cattedrale di San Giovanni Evangelista** (Duomo di Sansepolcro; Via Giacomo Matteotti 4; ⌚10am-noon & 4-7pm), which contains an *Ascension* by Perugino. The highlight, though, is the **Museo Civico** (☎0575 73 22 18; www.museocivicosansepolcro.it; Via Niccolò Aggiunti 65; adult/reduced €10/8.50, with Casa di Piero della Francesca €11/9.50; ⌚10am-1.30pm & 2.30-6.40pm mid-Jun–mid-Sep, 10am-1pm & 2.30-5.40pm mid-Sep–mid-Jun), whose small but top-notch collection includes della Francesca's *Resurrection* (1458–74) and *Madonna della Misericordia* (Madonna of Mercy) polyptych (1445–56) as well as two fresco fragments portraying *San Ludovico* (Saint Ludovic; 1460) and *San Giuliano* (Saint Julian; 1460).

The Drive » Head southwest from Sansepolcro along the SS73 following signs for Arezzo. After roughly 12km of easy driving through pleasant green countryside, turn left onto the SP42 and continue for 3km to Monterchi. It takes about 25 minutes.

BELA TOROK/500PX ©

4 Monterchi

This unassuming village has one of Piero della Francesca's best-loved works, the *Madonna del parto* (Pregnant Madonna; c 1460). Housed in its own museum, the **Museo della Madonna del Parto** (Pregnant Madonna Museum; ☎0575 7 07 13; www.madonnadelparto.it; Via della Reglia 1; adult/reduced €6.50/5; ⌚9am-1pm & 2-7pm Apr-Oct, to 5pm Wed-Mon Nov-Mar), it depicts a heavily pregnant Madonna wearing a simple blue gown and standing in a tent, flanked by two angels who hold back the tent's curtains as a framing device. In a nice touch, pregnant women get free entry to the museum.

The Drive » Take the SP221 out of Monterchi until you hit the SS73. Turn left and follow the fast-running road, which opens to four lanes in certain tracts, as it snakes through thickly wooded hills up to Arezzo.

TRIP HIGHLIGHT

5 Arezzo (p69)

The biggest town in eastern Tuscany, Arezzo has a distinguished cultural history. Italian poet Petrarch and art historian Giorgio Vasari were both born here, and, between

PIERO DELLA FRANCESCA

Though many details about his life are hazy, it's believed that Piero della Francesca was born around 1415 in Sansepolcro and died in 1492. Trained as a painter from the age of 15, his distinctive use of perspective, mastery of light and skilful synthesis of form and colour set him apart from his artistic contemporaries. His most famous works are the *Leggenda della Vera Croce* (Legend of the True Cross) in Arezzo, and *Resurrezione* (Resurrection) in Sansepolcro, but he is most fondly remembered for his luminous *Madonna del parto* (Pregnant Madonna) in Monterchi.

Arezzo Piazza Grande

1452 and 1466, Piero della Francesca painted one of his greatest works, the *Leggenda della Vera Croce* (Legend of the True Cross) fresco cycle in the Basilica di San Francesco's **Cappella Bacci** (☎0575 35 27 27; www.pierodellafrancesca.it; Piazza San Francesco; adult/reduced €8/5; ⏰9am-6pm Mon-Fri, to 5.30pm Sat, 1-5.30pm Sun, extended hours summer).

Once you've seen that, take time to admire the magnificent Romanesque facade of the **Chiesa di Santa Maria della Pieve** (Corso Italia 7; ⏰8am-12.30pm & 3-6.30pm) en route to the **Duomo** (Cattedrale di SS Donato e Pietro; Piazza del Duomo; ⏰7am-12.30pm & 3-6.30pm) and yet another della Francesca fresco – his *Mary Magdalene* (c 1460).

Film buffs should also stop by **Piazza Grande**, where scenes were filmed for Roberto Benigni's *La vita è bella* (Life is Beautiful), and where the city celebrates its big annual festival, the **Giostra del Saracino** (Joust of the Saracino), on the third or fourth Saturday of June and the first Sunday of September.

The Drive » The quickest route to Florence is via the A1 autostrada, but you'll enjoy the scenery more if you follow the SR71 up the Casentino valley and on to the medieval castle town of Poppi. At Poppi pick up the SR70 to tackle the heavily forested Passo della Consuma (1050m) and descend to Pontassieve and the SS67 into Florence. Allow about 2¾ hours.

TRIP HIGHLIGHT

6 Florence (p52)

The last port of call is Florence, the city where the Renaissance kicked off in the late 14th century. Paying the way was the Medici family, who sponsored the great artists of the day and whose

THE RENAISSANCE

Bridging the gap between the Middle Ages and the modern world, the Renaissance *(il Rinascimento)* emerged in 14th-century Florence and quickly spread throughout Italy.

The Early Days

Giotto di Bondone (1267–1337) is generally considered the first great Renaissance artist, and with his exploration of perspective and a new interest in realistic portraiture, he inspired artists such as Lorenzo Ghiberti (1378–1455) and Donatello (c 1382–1466). In architectural terms, the key man was Filippo Brunelleschi (1377–1446), whose dome on Florence's Duomo was one of the era's blockbuster achievements. Of the following generation, Sandro Botticelli (c 1444–1510) was a major player and his *Birth of Venus* (c 1485) was one of the most successful attempts to resolve the great conundrum of the age – how to give a painting both a realistic perspective and a harmonious composition.

The High Renaissance

By the early 16th century, the focus had shifted to Rome and Venice. Leading the way in Rome was Donato Bramante (1444–1514), whose classical architectural style greatly influenced the Veneto-born Andrea Palladio (1508–80). One of Bramante's great rivals was Michelangelo Buonarrotti (1475–1564), whose legendary genius was behind the Sistine Chapel frescoes, the dome over St Peter's Basilica, and the *David* sculpture. Other headline acts included Leonardo da Vinci (1452–1519), who developed a painting technique (sfumato) enabling him to modulate his contours using colour; and Raphael (1483–1520), who more than any other painter mastered the art of depicting large groups of people in a realistic and harmonious way.

collection today graces the **Galleria degli Uffizi** (Uffizi Gallery; ☎055 29 48 83; www.uffizi.it; Piazzale degli Uffizi 6; adult/reduced Mar-Oct €20/10, Nov-Feb €12/6; ⏰8.15am-6.50pm Tue-Sun). Here you can admire Piero della Francesca's famous portrait of the red-robed *Duke and Duchess of Urbino* (1465–72) alongside works by Renaissance giants, from Giotto and Cimabue to Botticelli, Leonardo da Vinci, Raphael and Titian.

Elsewhere in town, you'll find spiritually uplifting works by Fra' Angelico in the wonderful **Museo di San Marco** (☎055 238 86 08; Piazza San Marco 3; adult/reduced €4/2; ⏰8.15am-1.50pm Mon-Fri, to 4.50pm Sat & Sun, closed 1st, 3rd & 5th Sun, 2nd & 4th Mon of month), and superb frescoes by Masaccio, Masolino da Panicale and Filippino Lippi at the **Cappella Brancacci** (☎055 238 21 95; www.museicivicifiorentini.comune.fi.it; Piazza del Carmine 14; adult/reduced Wed-Fri €8/6, Sat-Mon €10/7; ⏰10am-5pm Wed-Sat & Mon, 1-5pm Sun), over the river in the Basilica di Santa Maria del Carmine. The historic centre is a great place to explore on foot (p61).

Urbino Palazzo Ducale (p37)

EVADEB/SHUTTERSTOCK ©

Monasteries of Tuscany & Umbria

This trip takes in world-famous basilicas, remote hermitages and secluded sanctuaries as it leads from Assisi to a 15th-century Florentine monastery frescoed by Fra' Angelico.

TRIP HIGHLIGHTS

262 km

Museo di San Marco
Exquisite frescoes in a 15th-century monastery

7 FINISH

Poppi

4

150 km

Santuario della Verna
Remote sanctuary in stunning surroundings

Arezzo

75 km

3

Cortona & Eremo Francescano Le Celle
A classic Tuscan hilltop town and hermitage

Perugia

START 1

0 km

Assisi
Fabulous church art in St Francis' hometown

5 DAYS
262KM / 163 MILES

GREAT FOR...

BEST TIME TO GO

Summer and early autumn are best for monastic visits.

ESSENTIAL PHOTO

The towered castle at Poppi.

BEST FOR HIKING

The forests around the Santuario della Verna.

Assisi Basilica di San Francesco (p44)

4 Monasteries of Tuscany & Umbria

Away from the crowds and bright lights, an austere 11th-century monastery sits in silence surrounded by forest and rocky mountainsides. Welcome to the Monastero & Sacro Eremo di Camaldoli, one of the starkly beautiful monasteries that you'll discover on this tour of central Umbria and Tuscany. Most people don't venture into the remote and densely forested locations where these monasteries are set, but they set the scene for a gripping drive.

TRIP HIGHLIGHT

1 Assisi (p90)

Both the birthplace and the final resting place of St Francis, this medieval hilltop town is a major destination for millions of pilgrims. Its biggest drawcard is the **Basilica di San Francesco** (www.sanfrancescoassisi.org; Piazza Superiore di San Francesco; ⌚basilica superiore 8.30am-6.50pm, basilica inferiore 6am-6.50pm summer, shorter hours winter), which comprises two gloriously frescoed

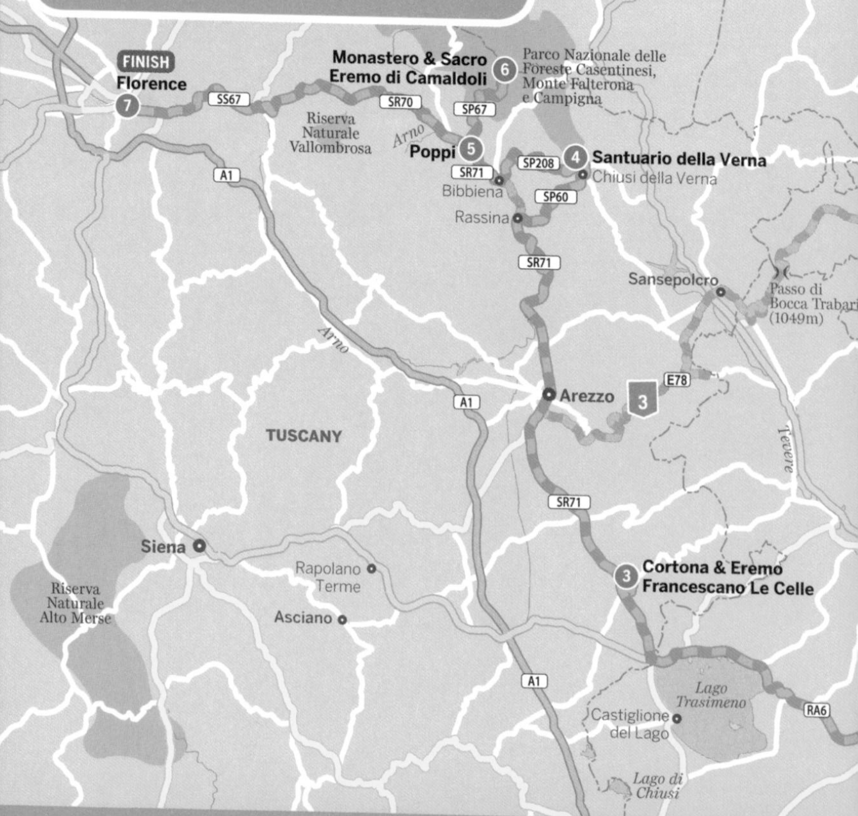

churches – the Gothic **Basilica Superiore** (upper church), which was built between 1230 and 1253 and features a celebrated fresco cycle by Giotto, and the dimly lit **Basilica Inferiore** (lower church), with frescoes by Simone Martini, Cimabue and Pietro Lorenzetti.

At the other end of the *centro storico* (historic centre), the 13th-century **Basilica di Santa Chiara** (www.assisisantachiara.it; Piazza Santa Chiara; ⏲6.30am-noon & 2-7pm summer, to 6pm winter) is the last resting place of St Clare, a contemporary of St Francis and founder of the Order of the Poor Ladies, aka the Poor Clares.

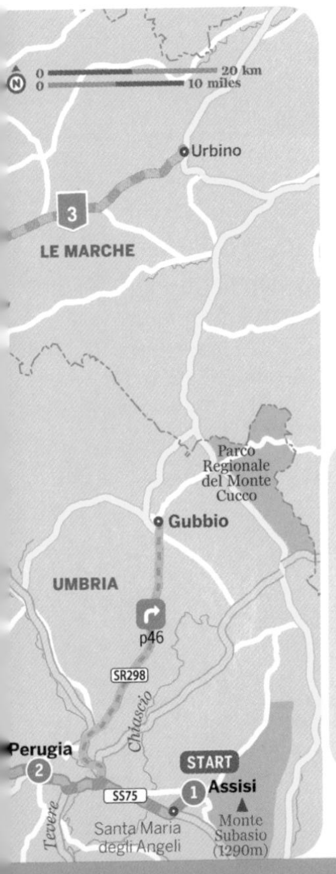

The Drive » From Assisi you can get to Perugia in about 40 minutes, but if you've got time it's worth stopping off to admire the basilica at Santa Maria degli Angeli. From Assisi head down the snaking road to Santa Maria degli Angeli and pick up the fast-running SS75 to Perugia.

❷ Perugia (p94)

With its hilltop medieval centre and international student population, Perugia is as close as Umbria gets to a heaving metropolis – which isn't all that close. Action is focused on the main strip, **Corso Vannucci**, and **Piazza IV Novembre**, home to the austere 14th-century **Cattedrale di San Lorenzo** (☎075 572 38 32; Piazza IV Novembre; ⏲7.30am-12.30pm & 3.30-6.45pm Mon-Sat, 8am-12.45pm & 4-7pm Sun) with its unfinished two-tone facade.

LINK YOUR TRIP

3 Piero della Francesca Trail

Push north from Cortona to Arezzo and join up with this art-based trail that runs from Urbino to Florence.

Over the square, the 13th-century **Palazzo dei Priori** houses Perugia's best museums, including the **Galleria Nazionale dell'Umbria** (☎075 572 10 09; www.gallerianazionaleumbria.it; Palazzo dei Priori, Corso Vannucci 19; adult/reduced €8/4; ⏲8.30am-7.30pm Tue-Sun year-round, plus from noon Mon mid-Mar–Oct), with a collection containing works by local heroes Perugino and Pinturicchio. Close to the *palazzo* (mansion), the impressive **Nobile Collegio del Cambio** (Exchange Hall; ☎075 572 85 99; www.collegiodelcambio.it; Palazzo dei Priori, Corso Vannucci 25; €4.50, incl Nobile Collegio della Mercanzia €5.50; ⏲9am-12.30pm & 2.30-5.30pm Mon-Sat, 9am-1pm Sun) also has some wonderful frescoes by Perugino.

The Drive » From Perugia it's just under an hour's drive to Cortona. Pick up the RA6 Raccordo Autostradale Bettolle-Perugia and head west, skirting Lago Trasimeno before joining the northbound SR71 at the lake's northwestern corner. From there the pace slackens as the road cuts through vineyards and sunflower fields up to Cortona.

TRIP HIGHLIGHT

❸ Cortona (p73) & Eremo Francescano Le Celle

A stunning hilltop town, and the setting for the film *Under the Tuscan Sun*, Cortona has a remarkable artistic

DETOUR: GUBBIO

Start: 2 Perugia

Stacked on the steep slopes of an Umbrian mountainside, the medieval town of Gubbio is well worth a visit. Highlights include **Piazza Grande**, with grandstand views over the surrounding countryside, and the **Museo Civico Palazzo dei Consoli** (☎075 927 42 98; www.palazzodeiconsoli.it; Palazzo dei Consoli, Piazza Grande; adult/reduced €10/5; ⊙10am-1pm & 3-6pm Mon-Fri, 10am-6pm Sat & Sun, shorter hours winter), where you'll find Gubbio's most famous treasures – the Iguvine Tablets. Dating to between 300 BC and 100 BC, these bronze tablets are inscribed with ancient text, the finest existing samples of the ancient Umbrian language.

For a change of scene, and yet more views, take the **Funivia Colle Eletto** (☎075 927 38 81; www.funiviagubbio.it; Via San Girolamo; adult/reduced one way €4/3, return €6/4; ⊙9am-8pm daily Jul & Aug, shorter hours rest of year) up to the **Basilica di Sant'Ubaldo** high above on Monte Ingino.

Gubbio is just over an hour's drive northeast of Perugia on the SR298.

MARTIN HUGHES/LONELY PLANET ©

pedigree. Fra' Angelico lived and worked here in the late 14th century, and fellow artists Luca Signorelli and Pietro da Cortona were both born within its walls – all three are represented in the excellent **Museo Diocesano di Arte Sacra** (☎0575 6 28 30; Piazza del Duomo 1; adult/reduced €5/3; ⊙10am-6.30pm daily Apr-Oct, 11am-4pm Tue-Fri, 10am-5pm Sat & Sun Nov-Mar).

Three kilometres north of town in dense woodland, the Franciscan hermitage called **Eremo Francescano Le Celle** (☎0575 60 33 62; Strada dei Cappuccini 1; ⊙7am-7pm) sits next to a picturesque stream. It's a wonderfully tranquil spot, disturbed only by the bells calling the resident friars to mass in the cave-like **Chiesa Cella di San Francesco**.

The Drive » The 1¾-hour drive to the Santuario della Verna takes you deep into the heart of the Casentino hills. From Cortona head north on the SR71. About 25km beyond Arezzo, in Rassina, follow signs right and continue up the densely wooded slopes to Chiusi della Verna. The sanctuary is about 3km above Chiusi.

TRIP HIGHLIGHT

4 Santuario della Verna

St Francis of Assisi is said to have received the stigmata at the **Santuario della Verna** (☎0575 53 41; www.laverna.it; Via del Santuario 45, Chiusi della Verna; ⊙sanctuary 6.30am-10pm summer, to 7.30pm winter, Cappella delle Stimmate 8am-7pm summer, to 5pm winter, Museo della Verna 10am-noon & 1-4pm Sat & Sun, daily Jul & Aug) on the southeastern edge of the **Parco Nazionale delle Foreste Casentinesi Monte Fal-**

Florence Fresco in Museo di San Marco (p48)

terona e Campigna (www.parcoforestecasentinesi.it). The sanctuary, which is dramatically positioned on a windswept mountainside, holds some fine glazed ceramics by Andrea della Robbia and his studio, including a magnificent *Crucifixion* in the **Cappella delle Stimmate**, the 13th-century chapel built on the spot where the saint supposedly received the stigmata.

The Drive » Allow about 45 minutes to Poppi from the sanctuary. The first leg, along the SP208, winds through the lush tree-covered mountains to Bibbiena, from where it's an easy 5km north on the SR71. You'll know you're near when you see Poppi's castle up on your left.

5 Poppi (p71)

Perched high above the Arno plain, Poppi is crowned by the **Castello dei Conti Guidi** (☎0575 52 05 16; www.buonconte.com; Piazza della Repubblica 1; adult/reduced €7/4; ⏰10am-4.30pm Thu-Sun, extended hours summer). Inside the 13th-century structure, you'll find a fairy-tale courtyard, a library full of medieval manuscripts, and a chapel with frescoes by Taddeo Gaddi, including a gruesome depiction of *Herod's Feast* with a dancing Salome and headless John the Baptist.

The Drive » Camaldoli is about 13km from Poppi. Take the SP67 (Via Camaldoli) and follow it up through the forest until you come to a fork in the road – the hermitage is uphill to the right; the monastery is downhill to the left.

6 Monastero & Sacro Eremo di Camaldoli

The 11th-century **Sacro Eremo e Monastero di Camaldoli** (Camaldoli Hermitage & Monastery;

ST FRANCIS OF ASSISI

The son of a wealthy merchant and a French noblewoman, Francesco was born in Assisi in 1181. He enjoyed a carefree youth, but in his mid-20s he went off to fight against Perugia and spent a year in an enemy prison. Illness followed and after a series of holy visions he decided to renounce his possessions and live a humble life in imitation of Christ, preaching and helping the poor. He travelled widely, performing miracles (curing the sick, communicating with animals) and establishing monasteries until his death in 1226. He was canonised two years later.

Today, various places claim links with the saint, including Gubbio where he supposedly brokered a deal between the townsfolk and a man-eating wolf, and Rome where Pope Innocent III allowed him to found the Franciscan order at the Basilica di San Giovanni in Laterano.

(☎Monastery 0575 55 60 12, hermitage 0575 55 60 21; www.camaldoli.it; Località Camaldoli 14, Camal-doli; ⏲hermitage 6-11am & 3-6pm, monastery 8am-noon & 2.30-6pm, pharmacy 9am-12.30pm & 2-6pm) sits immersed in thick forest on the southern fringes of the Parco Nazionale delle Foreste Casentinesi Monte Falterona e Campigna. Home to a small group of Benedictine monks, it has some wonderful art. In the monastery's **church** you'll find three paintings by Vasari: *Deposition from the Cross; Virgin with Child, St John the Baptist and St Girolamo;* and a Nativity. At the hermitage, the small church harbours an exquisite altarpiece by Andrea della Robbia.

For a souvenir, pop into the 16th-century **pharmacy** and pick up soap, perfumes and other items made by the resident monks.

The Drive » From the Monastero di Camaldoli, it's a 1½-hour drive to the Florentine monastery now housing the Museo di San Marco. From Camaldoli, double back along the SP67 and then head west along the SR70 through Poppi and then over the Passo della Consuma, a scenic mountain pass in the Tuscan section of the Appenine mountains, before following the river Arno through Pontassieve and into Florence's historic centre.

TRIP HIGHLIGHT

7 Museo di San Marco, Florence (p52)

This 15th-century Dominican monastery located next to the Chiesa di San Marco in the Florentine neighbourhhod of the same name is one of the city's most spiritually uplifting **museums** (☎055 238 86 08; Piazza San Marco 3; adult/reduced €4/2; ⏲8.15am-1.50pm Mon-Fri, to 4.50pm Sat & Sun, closed 1st, 3rd & 5th Sun, 2nd & 4th Mon of month), showcasing frescoes by Fra' Angelico ('Il Beato Angelico'; The Blessed Angelic One), an artist and monk who was made a saint by Pope John Paul II in 1984. Major works here include Fra' Angelico's haunting *Annunciation* (c 1440) on the staircase leading to the monks' cells, one of the best-loved of all Renaissance artworks.

Perugia Piazza IV Novembre and Cattedrale di San Lorenzo (p45)

ARTMEDIAFACTORY/SHUTTERSTOCK ©

Destinations

Florence & Eastern Tuscany (p52)

Florence is a city buzzing with romance and history, set in a region of gently rolling hills, sun-kissed vineyards and avenues of cypress trees.

Siena & Southern Tuscany (p74)

Beautifully preserved, medieval Siena crowns a region that produces some of Italy's most famous wines.

Assisi & Umbria (p90)

With the plains spreading picturesquely below and Monte Subasio rearing above, the home of St Francis welcomes pilgrims.

Val d'Orcia (p84)

BLUEJAYPHOTO/GETTY IMAGES ©

Florence & Eastern Tuscany

Cradle of the Renaissance and home of Machiavelli, Michelangelo and the Medici, Florence is magnetic, romantic and brilliantly absorbing.

FLORENCE

☎055 / POP 382,250

Return time and again and you still won't see it all. Stand on a bridge over the Arno river several times in a day and the light, mood and view change every time. Surprisingly small as it is, Florence (Firenze) looms large on Europe's 'must-see' list. Host to the tourist masses that flock here to feast on world-class art, Tuscany's largest city buzzes with romance and history. Towers and palaces evoke a thousand tales of its medieval past; designer boutiques and artisan workshops pearl its streets; and the local drinking and dining scene is second to none.

Sights

Florence's wealth of museums and galleries house many of the world's most exquisite examples of Renaissance art, and its architecture is unrivalled. Yet don't feel pressured to see everything: combine your personal pick of sights with ample meandering through the city's warren of narrow streets broken by cafe and *enoteca* (wine bar) stops.

Churches enforce a strict dress code for visitors: no shorts, sleeveless shirts or plunging necklines. Photography with no flash is allowed in museums, but leave the selfie stick at home – they are officially forbidden.

★Duomo CATHEDRAL

(Cattedrale di Santa Maria del Fiore; Map p56; ☎055 230 28 85; www.museumflorence.com; Piazza del Duomo; ⌚10am-5pm Mon-Wed & Fri, to 4.30pm Thu & Sat, 1.30-4.45pm Sun) FREE Florence's *duomo* is the city's most iconic landmark. Capped by Filippo Brunelleschi's red-tiled **cupola** (Brunelleschi's Dome; adult/reduced incl baptistry, campanile, crypt & museum €18/3), it's a staggering construction whose breathtaking pink, white and green marble facade and graceful **campanile** (Bell Tower) dominate the Renaissance cityscape. Sienese architect Arnolfo di Cambio began work on it in 1296, but construction took almost 150 years and it wasn't consecrated until 1436. In the echoing interior, look out for frescoes by Vasari and Zuccari and up to 44 stained-glass windows.

Piazza della Signoria PIAZZA

(Map p56) The hub of local life since the 13th century, where Florentines flock to meet friends and chat over early-evening *aperitivi* (predinner drinks) at historic cafes. Presiding over everything is **Palazzo Vecchio**, Florence's city hall, and the 14th-century **Loggia dei Lanzi**.

★Galleria degli Uffizi GALLERY

(Uffizi Gallery; Map p56; ☎055 29 48 83; www.uffizi.it; Piazzale degli Uffizi 6; adult/reduced Mar-Oct €20/10, Nov-Feb €12/6; ⌚8.15am-6.50pm Tue-Sun) Home to the world's greatest collection of Italian Renaissance art, Florence's premier gallery occupies the vast U-shaped Palazzo degli Uffizi (1560–80), built as government offices. The collection, bequeathed to the city

Florence

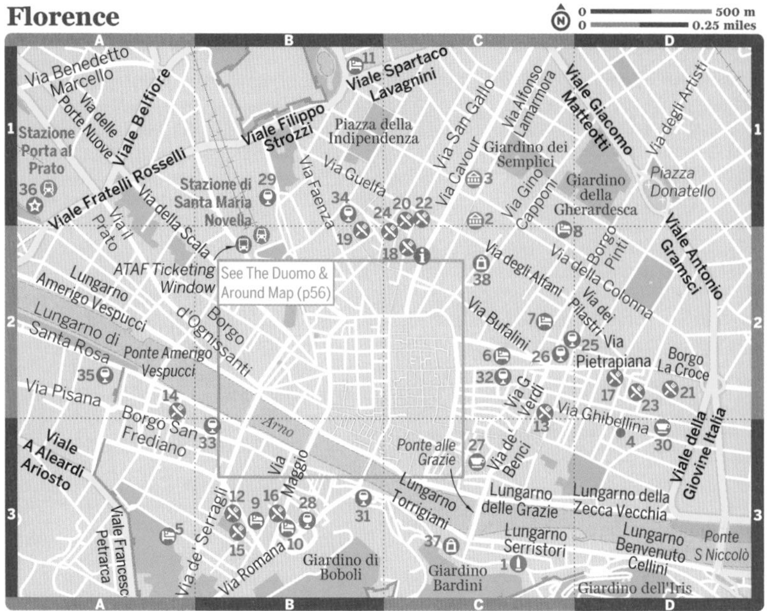

Florence

Sights
1 Clet ... C3
2 Galleria dell'Accademia ... C1
3 Museo di San Marco ... C1

Activities, Courses & Tours
4 Tuscany Bike Tours ... D3

Sleeping
5 AdAstra ... A3
6 Hotel Dalí ... C2
7 Hotel Monna Lisa ... C2
8 Hotel Morandi alla Crocetta ... C2
9 Hotel Palazzo Guadagni ... B3
10 SoprArno Suites ... B3
11 Student Hotel ... B1

Eating
12 #Raw ... B3
13 Enoteca Pinchiorri ... C2
14 Essenziale ... A2
15 Gurdulù ... B3
16 Gustapizza ... B3
17 Il Teatro del Sale ... D2
18 La Ménagère ... C2
19 Mercato Centrale ... B2
20 My Sugar ... C1
21 Santarpia ... D2
22 SimBIOsi ... C1
23 Terrazza Menoni ... D2
24 Trattoria Mario ... C2

Drinking & Nightlife
25 Bitter Bar ... C2
26 Buca 10 ... C2
27 Ditta Artigianale ... C3
28 Enoteca Pitti Gola e Cantina ... B3
29 Fabbricato Viaggiatori ... B1
30 Le Murate ... D3
31 Le Volpi e l'Uva ... B3
32 Locale ... C2
33 Mad Souls & Spirits ... B3
34 PanicAle ... B1
35 Santarosa Bistrot ... A2

Entertainment
36 Teatro del Maggio Musicale Fiorentino ... A1

Shopping
37 Lorenzo Villoresi ... C3
38 Street Doing ... C2

by the Medici family in 1743 on condition that it never leave Florence, contains some of Italy's best-known paintings, including a room full of Botticelli masterpieces.

A combined ticket (valid three days) with Palazzo Pitti, Giardino di Boboli and Museo Archeologico is available for €38/21 (€18/11 November to February).

Chiesa e Museo di Orsanmichele CHURCH
(Map p56; Via dell'Arte della Lana; ⌚church 10am-4.50pm daily, closed Mon Aug, museum 10am-4.50pm Mon, 10am-12.30pm Sat) FREE This unusual and inspirational church, with a Gothic tabernacle by Andrea Orcagna, was created when the arcades of an old grain market (1290) were walled in and two storeys added during the 14th century. Its exterior is decorated with niches and tabernacles bearing statues representing the patron saints of Florence's many guilds, commissioned in the 15th and 16th centuries after the *signoria* (city government) ordered the guilds to finance the church's decoration.

★**Museo del Bargello** MUSEUM
(Map p56; ☎055 238 86 06; www.bargellomusei.beniculturali.it; Via del Proconsolo 4; adult/reduced €8/4; ⌚8.15am-2pm, closed 2nd & 4th Sun, 1st, 3rd & 5th Mon of month) It was behind the stark walls of Palazzo del Bargello, Florence's earliest public building, that the *podestà* (governing magistrate) meted out justice from the 13th century until 1502. Today the building safeguards Italy's most comprehensive collection of Tuscan Renaissance sculpture, with some of Michelangelo's best early works and several by Donatello. Michelangelo was just 21 when a cardinal commissioned him to create the drunken grape-adorned *Bacchus* (1496–97). Unfortunately the cardinal didn't like the result and sold it.

TIME SAVER

The **Firenze Card** (www.firenzecard.it; €85) is valid for 72 hours and covers admission to 70-plus museums, villas and gardens in Florence, as well as unlimited use of public transport and free wi-fi across the city. To add on unlimited public transport, pay an additional €7 for a Firenzecard+ add-on. The card's biggest advantage is reducing queueing time in high season – museums have a separate queue for card-holders. The downside of the Firenze Card is it only allows one admission per museum, plus you need to visit an awful lot of museums to justify the cost. Buy the card online (and collect upon arrival in Florence or download the Firenze Card App and store it digitally).

★**Basilica di Santa Maria Novella** BASILICA
(Map p56; ☎055 21 92 57; www.smn.it; Piazza di Santa Maria Novella 18; adult/reduced €7.50/5; ⌚9am-7pm Mon-Thu, 11am-7pm Fri, 9am-6.30pm Sat, noon-6.30pm Sun Jul & Aug, shorter hours rest of year) The striking green-and-white marble facade of 13th- to 15th-century Basilica di Santa Maria Novella fronts an entire monastical complex, comprising romantic church cloisters and a frescoed chapel. The basilica itself is a treasure chest of artistic masterpieces, climaxing with frescoes by Domenico Ghirlandaio. The lower section of the basilica's striped marbled facade is transitional from Romanesque to Gothic; the upper section and the main doorway (1456–70) were designed by Leon Battista Alberti. Book in advance online to avoid queues.

★**Museo Novecento** MUSEUM
(Museum of the 20th Century; Map p56; ☎055 28 61 32; www.museonovecento.it; Piazza di Santa Maria Novella 10; adult/reduced €9.50/4.50; ⌚11am-8pm Sat-Wed, to 2pm Thu, to 11pm Fri summer, 11am-7pm Fri-Wed, to 2pm Thu winter) Don't allow the Renaissance to distract you from Florence's fantastic modern art museum, at home in a 13th-century pilgrim shelter, hospital and school. A well-articulated itinerary guides visitors through modern Italian painting and sculpture from the early 20th century to the late 1980s. Installation art makes effective use of the outside space on the 1st-floor loggia. Fashion and theatre also get a nod, and the itinerary ends with a 20-minute cinematic montage of the best films set in Florence.

★**Galleria dell'Accademia** GALLERY
(Map p53; ☎055 238 86 09; www.galleriaaccademiafirenze.beniculturali.it; Via Ricasoli 60; adult/reduced €12/6; ⌚8.15am-6.50pm Tue-Sun) A queue marks the door to this gallery, built to house one of the Renaissance's most iconic masterpieces, Michelangelo's *David*. But the world's most famous statue is worth the wait. The subtle detail – the veins in his sinewy arms, the leg muscles, the change in expression as you move around the statue – *is* impressive. Carved from a single block of marble, Michelangelo's most famous work was his most challenging – he didn't choose the marble himself and it was veined.

★**Basilica di San Lorenzo** BASILICA
(Map p56; ☎055 21 40 42; www.operamedicealaurenziana.org; Piazza San Lorenzo; €6, with

MATEJ KASTELIC/SHUTTERSTOCK ©

Galleria degli Uffizi (p52)

Biblioteca Medicea Laurenziana €8.50; ⌚10am-5.30pm Mon-Sat) Considered one of Florence's most harmonious examples of Renaissance architecture, this unfinished basilica was the Medici parish church and mausoleum. It was designed by Brunelleschi in 1425 for Cosimo the Elder and built over a 4th-century church. In the solemn interior, look for Brunelleschi's austerely beautiful **Sagrestia Vecchia** (Old Sacristy) with its sculptural decoration by Donatello. Michelangelo was commissioned to design the facade in 1518, but his design in white Carrara marble was never executed, hence the building's rough, unfinished appearance.

★Museo di San Marco MUSEUM
(Map p53; ☎055 238 86 08; Piazza San Marco 3; adult/reduced €8/2; ⌚8.15am-1.50pm Mon-Fri, to 4.50pm Sat & Sun, closed 1st, 3rd & 5th Sun, 2nd & 4th Mon of month) At the heart of Florence's university area sits **Chiesa di San Marco** and an adjoining 15th-century Dominican monastery where both gifted painter Fra' Angelico (c 1395–1455) and the sharp-tongued Savonarola piously served God. Today the monastery, aka one of Florence's most spiritually uplifting museums, showcases the work of Fra' Angelico. After centuries of being known as 'Il Beato Angelico' (literally 'The Blessed Angelic One') or simply 'Il Beato' (The Blessed), the Renaissance's most blessed religious painter was made a saint by Pope John Paul II in 1984.

Ponte Vecchio BRIDGE
(Map p56) Dating from 1345, iconic Ponte Vecchio was the only Florentine bridge to survive destruction at the hands of retreating German forces in 1944. Above jewellery shops on the eastern side, the **Corridoio Vasariano** (Vasari Corridor; guided visit by reservation Mar-Oct €45, Nov-Feb €20) is a 16th-century passageway between the Uffizi and Palazzo Pitti that runs around, rather than through, the medieval **Torre dei Mannelli** at the bridge's southern end.

Tours

Curious Appetite TOURS
(☎391 4005956; www.curiousappetitetravel.com; 3hr group tour per person €85) Personalised bespoke and small-group culinary tours and tastings led by Italian-American Coral Sisk and her team of knowledgeable guides, most of whom are trained sommeliers too. Tours are themed: at the market, *aperitivi*, Italian food and wine pairings, 'dinner crawl', gelato etc. Cocktail lessons too with a Florentine mixologist.

Tuscany Bike Tours CYCLING
(Map p53; ☎339 1163495, 055 386 02 53; www.tuscany-biketours.com; Via Ghibellina 34r) Cycling tours in and around Florence, including a 2½-hour city bike tour with gelato break (adult/reduced €39/35) and a full-day bike ride into the Chianti hills (adult/reduced €85/75). For the less energetic,

The Duomo & Around

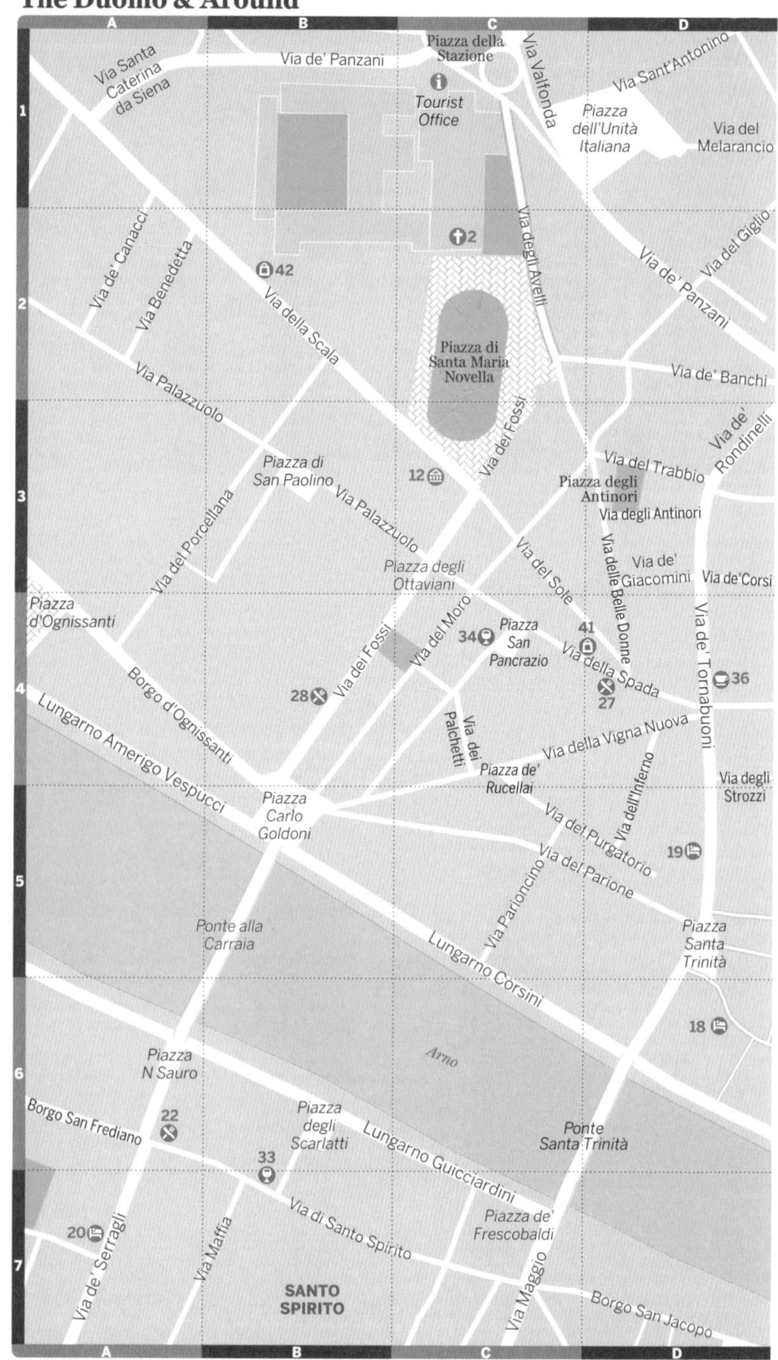

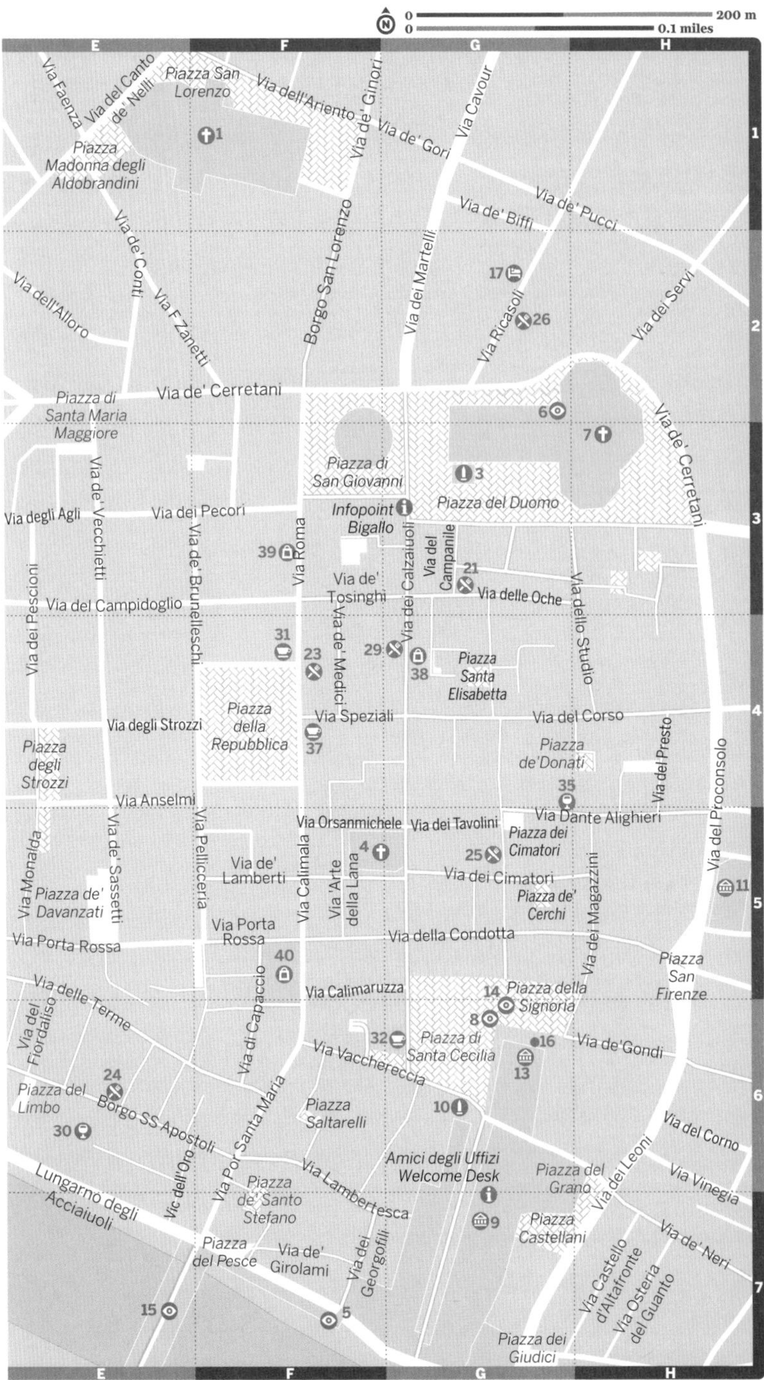
0 200 m
0 0.1 miles
E
F
G
H
1
2
3
4
5
6
7
Via Faenza
Via del Canto de' Nelli
Piazza San Lorenzo
Via dell'Ariento
Via de' Ginori
Via de' Gori
Via Cavour
Piazza Madonna degli Aldobrandini
Via de' Pucci
Via de' Biffi
Via de' Conti
Borgo San Lorenzo
Via dei Martelli
Via dell'Alloro
Via F Zanetti
Via Ricasoli
Via dei Servi
Via de' Cerretani
Piazza di Santa Maria Maggiore
Piazza di San Giovanni
Piazza del Duomo
Infopoint Bigallo
Via de' Vecchietti
Via degli Agli
Via dei Pecori
Via de' Brunelleschi
Via Roma
Via de' Tosinghi
Via dei Calzaiuoli
Via del Campanile
Via delle Oche
Via dello Studio
Via dei Pescioni
Via del Campidoglio
Via de' Medici
Piazza Santa Elisabetta
Via degli Strozzi
Piazza della Repubblica
Via Speziali
Via del Corso
Piazza degli Strozzi
Piazza de' Donati
Via del Presto
Via del Proconsolo
Via Anselmi
Via Orsanmichele
Via dei Tavolini
Via Dante Alighieri
Piazza dei Cimatori
Via Monalda
Via de' Sassetti
Via Pellicceria
Via de' Lamberti
Via Calimala
Via 'Arte della Lana
Via dei Cimatori
Piazza de' Cerchi
Via dei Magazzini
Piazza de' Davanzati
Via Porta Rossa
Via della Condotta
Piazza San Firenze
Via delle Terme
Via di Capaccio
Via Calimaruzza
Piazza della Signoria
Via del Fiordaliso
Piazza di Santa Cecilia
Via de'Gondi
Via Vacchereccia
Piazza del Limbo
Borgo SS Apostoli
Por Santa Maria
Piazza Saltarelli
Via del Corno
Via dei Leoni
Amici degli Uffizi Welcome Desk
Piazza del Grano
Via Vinegia
Lungarno degli Acciaiuoli
Vic dell'Oro
Via Por Santa Maria
Piazza de' Santo Stefano
Via Lambertesca
Piazza Castellani
Via de' Neri
Piazza del Pesce
Via de' Girolami
Via dei Georgofili
Via Castello d'Altafronte
Via Osteria del Guanto
Piazza dei Giudici
1
3
4
5
6
7
8
9
10
11
13
14
15
16
17
21
23
24
25
26
29
30
31
32
35
37
38
39
40

The Duomo & Around

Sights
1 Basilica di San Lorenzo ... F1
2 Basilica di Santa Maria Novella ... C2
3 Campanile ... G3
4 Chiesa e Museo di Orsanmichele ... F5
5 Corridoio Vasariano ... F7
6 Cupola del Brunelleschi ... G2
7 Duomo ... H3
8 Fontana di Nettuno ... G6
9 Galleria degli Uffizi ... G7
10 Loggia dei Lanzi ... G6
11 Museo del Bargello ... H5
12 Museo Novecento ... C3
13 Palazzo Vecchio ... G6
14 Piazza della Signoria ... G6
15 Ponte Vecchio ... E7

Activities, Courses & Tours
16 Mus.e ... G6

Sleeping
17 Academy Hostel ... G2
18 Hotel Cestelli ... D6
19 Hotel Scoti ... D5
20 Oltrarno Splendid ... A7

Eating
Floret ... (see 39)
21 Grom ... G3
22 Il Santo Bevitore ... A6
23 Irene ... F4
24 Mangiafoco ... E6
25 Osteria Il Buongustai ... G5
26 Regina Bistecca ... G2
27 Trattoria Marione ... D4
28 UqBar ... B4
29 Venchi ... G4

Drinking & Nightlife
30 Amblé ... E6
31 Caffè Gilli ... F4
32 Caffè Rivoire ... G6
33 Gosh ... B7
34 Manifattura ... C4
35 Mayday Club ... G4
36 Procacci ... D4
37 Tosca & Nino ... F4

Shopping
38 Benheart ... G4
39 Luisa Via Roma ... F3
40 Mercato Nuovo ... F5
41 Mio Concept ... D4
42 Officina Profumo-Farmaceutica di Santa Maria Novella ... B2

consider a Chianti day trip by Audrey Hepburn-style scooter (adult/reduced/passenger €130/120/95, including lunch, castle visit and wine or olive-oil tasting) or Fiat 500 (driver/passenger €150/90, including lunch). Bike hire too.

Festivals & Events

Festa di Anna Maria Medici CULTURAL
(18 Feb) Florence's Feast of Anna Maria Medici marks the death in 1743 of the last Medici, Anna Maria Luisa de' Medici, with a costumed parade from Palazzo Vecchio to her tomb in the Cappelle Medicee.

Maggio Musicale Fiorentino PERFORMING ARTS
(www.maggiofiorentino.com; Apr-Jun) Italy's oldest arts festival features world-class performances of theatre, classical music, jazz, opera and dance. Events are staged at the **Teatro del Maggio Musicale Fiorentino** (Map p53; 055 200 12 78; Piazzale Vittorio Gui 1; box office 10am-6pm Mon-Sat) and other key venues across the city.

Festa di San Giovanni RELIGIOUS
(24 Jun) Florence celebrates its patron saint, John, with a *calcio storico* (historic football) match on Piazza di Santa Croce and fireworks over Piazzale Michelangelo.

Sleeping

Florence is unexpectedly small, rendering almost anywhere in the city centre convenient. Advance reservations are essential between Easter and September; winter ushers in some great deals for visitors.

Duomo & Piazza della Signoria

Hotel Cestelli HOTEL €
(Map p56; 055 21 42 13; www.hotelcestelli.com; Borgo SS Apostoli 25; d €100, s/d without bathroom €60/80; closed 2 weeks Jan & 10 days Aug;) Housed in a 12th-century *palazzo* (mansion) a stiletto-strut from fashionable Via de' Tornabuoni, this intimate eight-room hotel is a gem. Rooms reveal an understated style, tastefully combining polished antiques with spangly chandeliers, vintage art and silk screens. Owners Alessio and Asumi are a mine of local information and are happy to share their knowledge. No breakfast. Ask about the low-season discounts for longer stays.

★**Hotel Scoti** PENSION €€

(Map p56; ☎055 29 21 28; www.hotelscoti.com; Via de' Tornabuoni 7; d/tr €140/165; 📶) Wedged between designer boutiques on Florence's smartest shopping strip, this hidden *pensione* is a fabulous mix of old-fashioned charm and value for money. Its traditionally styled rooms are spread across the 2nd floor of a 16th-century *palazzo;* some have lovely rooftop views. Guests can borrow hairdryers, bottle openers etc, and the frescoed lounge (1780) is stunning. Optional breakfast €5 extra.

Santa Maria Novella

★**Student Hotel** HOSTEL €

(Map p53; ☎055 062 18 55; www.thestudenthotel.com; Viale Spartaco Lavagnini 70; s/d from €92/109; ❄@📶🏊) Designed for anyone with a fun 'student for life' spirit, this hostel-hotel hybrid embodies 21st-century living – in a historic *palazzo* from 1864. The sharp interior design throws in a shiny grand piano for guests to tinkle on, co-working spaces, break-out zones and bags of communal space. Rooms, shared kitchens, and the 360-degree city views from the rooftop pool, gym and sky bar are positively hedonistic.

San Lorenzo & San Marco

★**Academy Hostel** HOSTEL €

(Map p56; ☎055 239 86 65; www.academyhostel.eu; Via Ricasoli 9; dm €30-45, d €70-90; ❄@📶) This classy hostel – definitely not a party hostel – sits on the 1st floor of Baron Ricasoli's 17th-century *palazzo*. The inviting lobby, with books to browse, was once a theatre and is a comfy spot to chill on the sofa over TV or a DVD. Dorms sport four, five or six beds, high moulded ceilings and brightly coloured lockers.

Hotel Monna Lisa HOTEL €€

(Map p53; ☎055 247 97 51; www.monnalisa.it; Borgo Pinti 27; d €140-200; P📶; 🚌) At home in a Renaissance *palazzo* endowed with beautiful paintings and sculptures, Monna Lisa is one chic place. Its 45 rooms are old-world and four-star, but what really stuns are the communal spaces – the glorious loggia with painted ceiling; the period lounges; and the peaceful garden with gravel paths, jasmine and lime trees.

Hotel Morandi alla Crocetta BOUTIQUE HOTEL €€

(Map p53; ☎055 234 47 48; www.hotelmorandi.it; Via Laura 50; s/d €120/170; P❄📶) This medieval convent-turned-hotel away from the madding crowd in San Marco is a stunner. Rooms are refined and traditional in look – think antique furnishings, wood beams and oil paintings – with a quiet, old-world ambience. Pick of the bunch is frescoed room No 29, the former chapel.

Santa Croce

★**Hotel Dalí** HOTEL €

(Map p53; ☎055 234 07 06; www.hoteldali.com; Via dell'Oriuolo 17; d €95, s/d without bathroom €40/70; P📶) A warm welcome from hosts Marco and Samanta awaits at this lovely small hotel. A stone's throw from the *duomo,* it has 10 sunny rooms, some overlooking a leafy inner courtyard, decorated in a low-key modern way and equipped with kettles, coffee and tea. No breakfast, but – miraculous for central Florence – free parking in the rear courtyard. The icing on the cake is a trio of gorgeous self-catering apartments sleeping three, four or six.

Oltrarno

★**Oltrarno Splendid** B&B €€

(Map p56; ☎055 464 85 55; www.oltrarnosplendid.com; Via dei Serragli 7; d €160-240; @📶) Original frescoes and toile de Jouy wall

Duomo (p52)
GIVAGA/SHUTTERSTOCK

fabrics, decorative fireplaces and a wonderful collection of vintage curios create an enriching sense of home at this exquisite guesthouse – the latest on-trend creation by calligrapher Betty Soldi and partner Matteo. All 14 rooms enjoy romantic rooftop views of Florence, and the welcome from maître d' Alberto could not be warmer or more charming.

★ **AdAstra** B&B **€€€**
(Map p53; 055 075 06 02; www.adastraflorence.com; Via del Campuccio 53; d €280-350; reception 8.30am-7.30pm; P) There is no other address quite like it in Florence. Seductively at home in a 16th-century *palazzo* overlooking Europe's largest private walled garden, this uberchic guesthouse rocks. A creation of the talented British-Italian duo behind SoprArno Suites, AdAstra sports 14 beautiful rooms adorned with Betty Soldi's calligraphy, Matteo's vintage collectibles, claw-foot bathtubs and the odd 19th-century fresco or wooden herringbone floor.

★ **Hotel Palazzo Guadagni** HOTEL **€€€**
(Map p53; 055 265 83 76; www.palazzoguadagni.com; Piazza Santo Spirito 9; d/tr/q €250/270/310;) This romantic midrange hotel overlooking Florence's liveliest summertime square is legendary – Zeffirelli shot scenes from *Tea with Mussolini* here. Housed in an artfully revamped Renaissance palace, it has 15 spacious rooms with old-world high ceilings and the occasional fresco or fireplace (decorative today). In summer bartenders serve cocktails on the impossibly romantic loggia terrace with wicker chairs and predictably dreamy views.

Eating

Quality ingredients and simple execution are the hallmarks of Florentine cuisine, climaxing with the *bistecca alla fiorentina*, a huge slab of prime T-bone steak rubbed with tangy Tuscan olive oil, seared on the chargrill, garnished with salt and pepper and served beautifully *al sangue* (bloody). Be it dining in a traditional trattoria or contemporary, designer-chic space, quality is guaranteed.

Duomo & Piazza della Signoria

★ **Osteria Il Buongustai** OSTERIA **€**
(Map p56; 055 29 13 04; www.facebook.com/ibuongustaifirenze; Via dei Cerchi 15r; meals €15-20; 9.30am-3.30pm Mon-Sat) Run with breathtaking speed and grace by Laura and Lucia, 'The Gourmand' is unmissable. Lunchtimes heave with locals and savvy students who flock here to fill up on tasty Tuscan home cooking at a snip of other restaurant prices. The place is brilliantly no-frills – watch women in hair caps at work in the kitchen, share a table and pay in cash.

No credit cards.

Mangiafoco TUSCAN **€€**
(Map p56; 055 265 81 70; www.mangiafoco.com; Borgo SS Apostoli 26r; meals €40; noon-midnight) Aromatic truffles get full-page billing at this small and cosy *osteria* (casual tavern) with buttercup-yellow walls, cushioned seating and an exceptional wine list. Whether you are a hardcore truffle fiend or a truffle virgin, there is something for you here: steak topped with freshly shaved truffles in season, truffle *tagliatelle* (ribbon pasta) or a simple plate of mixed cheeses with sweet truffle honey.

★ **Irene** BISTRO **€€€**
(Map p56; 055 273 58 91; www.roccofortehotels.com; Piazza della Repubblica 7; meals €60; 7.30am-10.30pm) Named after the accomplished Italian grandmother of Sir Rocco Forte of the eponymous luxury hotel group, Irene (part of neighbouring Hotel Savoy) is a dazzling contemporary bistro with a pavement terrace (heated in winter) overlooking iconic Piazza della Repubblica. Interior design is retro-chic 1950s and celebrity chef Fulvio Pierangelini cooks up playful, utterly fabulous bistro cuisine.

Santa Maria Novella

★ **UqBar** CAFE **€**
(Todo Modo; Map p56; 055 239 91 10; www.todomodo.org; Via dei Fossi 15r; meals €15-25; 10am-8pm Tue-Sun, closed Sun May-Sep;) Grab a vintage pew between book- and bottle-lined shelves inside the city's most dynamic independent bookshop, select a glass of well-chosen wine, and tuck into a tasty 'slow food' lunch that changes daily. Outside of lunch hours (12.30pm to 3.30pm), enjoy fresh coffee and homemade cakes in the company of a good book. *Aperitivo*, from 6pm, is the other hot date.

Trattoria Marione TRATTORIA **€€**
(Map p56; 055 21 47 56; Via della Spada 27; meals €30; noon-5pm & 7-11pm) For the quintessential 'Italian dining' experience,

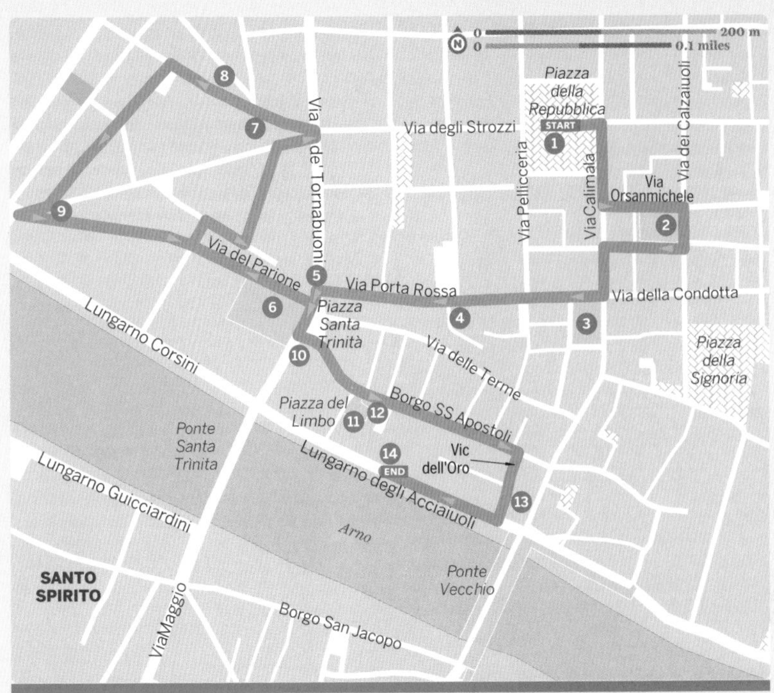

City Walk
Quintessential Florence

START PIAZZA DELLA REPUBBLICA
END LA TERAZZA LOUNGE BAR
LENGTH 2.5KM; TWO HOURS

Start with coffee on 1 **Piazza della Repubblica**, then walk one block south along Via Calimala and turn left onto Via Orsanmichele to 2 **Chiesa e Museo di Orsanmichele** (p54), a unique church with ornate statuary adorning its facade and a fascinating museum inside. Backtrack to Via Calimala and continue walking south until you see the loggia of 3 **Mercato Nuovo** (p67), the 16th-century 'New Market'. Florentines know it as 'Il Porcellino' (The Piglet) after the bronze statue of a wild boar on its southern side. Rub its snout to ensure your return to Florence.

Walk past the market and along Via Porta Rossa to 4 **Palazzo Davanzati** (Via Porta Rossa 13) with its magnificent studded doors and captivating museum.

Continue to 5 **Via de' Tornabuoni** with its luxury boutiques. Swoon over frescoed chapels in 6 **Chiesa di Santa Trìnita** (Piazza Santa Trinità), then lose yourself in the line-up of boutiques on Via del Parione, Via della Vigna Nuova and Via della Spada: milliner 7 **Grevi** (Via della Spada 11-13r), 8 **Mio Concept** (p68) packed with homewares and fashion accessories, and leather designer 9 **Benheart** (Via della Vigna Nuova 95-97r) are grass-root Florentine favourites.

Backtrack to Via de' Tornabuoni and turn right, past 13th-century 10 **Palazzo Spini-Feroni**, home of Salvatore Ferragamo's flagship store, to Borgo Santissimi Apostoli. A short way ahead on Piazza del Limbo is the Romanesque 11 **Chiesa dei Santissimi Apostoli**, once used as a cemetery for unbaptised babies.

After browsing for olive oil in 12 **La Bottega dell'Olio** (Piazza del Limbo 4r), continue east and turn right into Vicolo dell'Oro, home to the Hotel Continentale, whose sleek terrace rooftop 13 **La Terrazza Lounge Bar** (Vicolo dell'Oro 6r) is the perfect spot for a sundowner. If hipster Florence is more your cup of tea, indulge in an alfresco aperitivo at 14 **Amblé** (p64).

Marione is gold. It's busy, it's noisy, it's 99% local and the cuisine is right out of *nonna's* Tuscan kitchen. No one appears to speak English so go for Italian – the tasty excellent-value traditional fare is worth it. If you don't get a complimentary *limoncello* (lemon liqueur) with the bill, you clearly failed the language test.

San Lorenzo & San Marco

★Mercato Centrale FOOD HALL €
(Map p53; ☎055 239 97 98; www.mercatocentrale.it; Piazza del Mercato Centrale 4; dishes €5-15; ⏲market 7am-3pm Mon-Fri, to 5pm Sat, food hall 8am-midnight; 📶) Wander the maze of stalls crammed with fresh produce at Florence's oldest and largest food market, on the ground floor of an iron-and-glass structure designed by architect Giuseppe Mengoni in 1874. Head to the 1st floor's buzzing, thoroughly contemporary food hall with dedicated cookery school and artisan stalls cooking steaks, burgers, tripe *panini*, vegetarian dishes, pizza, gelato, pastries and pasta.

★Trattoria Mario TUSCAN €
(Map p53; ☎055 21 85 50; www.trattoria-mario.com; Via Rosina 2; meals €25; ⏲noon-3.30pm Mon-Sat, closed 3 weeks Aug; ❄) Arrive by noon to ensure a spot at this noisy, busy, brilliant trattoria – a legend that retains its soul (and allure with locals) despite being in every guidebook. Charming Fabio, whose grandfather opened the place in 1953, is front of house while big brother Romeo and nephew Francesco cook with speed in the kitchen. No advance reservations; cash only.

★La Ménagère INTERNATIONAL €€
(Map p53; ☎055 075 06 00; www.lamenagere.it; Via de' Ginori 8r; meals €15-70; ⏲7am-2am; 📶) Be it breakfast, lunch, dinner, coffee or cocktails, this industrial-styled space lures Florence's hip brigade. The concept store is a fashionable one-stop shop for chic china and tableware, designer kitchen gear and fresh flowers. For daytime dining, pick from retro sofas in the boutique, banquette seating or bar stools in the bistro or a table between flower pots in the conservatory-style restaurant.

★Regina Bistecca STEAK €€€
(Map p56; ☎055 269 37 72; www.reginabistecca.com; Via Ricasoli 14r; menus €25-59, meals €40-50; ⏲12.30-3pm & 7-10.30pm Tue-Sun; 📶) Plump for a high stool and beautifully mixed Negroni in the wood-panelled American bar, lined with bookshelves and vintage prints in homage to the space's former life as an antiquarian bookshop (since 1875). Or relax in the effortless elegance of the colonnaded, white-table-clothed restaurant where exquisitely cooked, charcoal-grilled steak reigns supreme.

Sunday ushers in a hog roast, and the dessert trolley at this fashionable steak house is Italian heaven on earth.

Santa Croce

★Terrazza Menoni STREET FOOD €
(Map p53; ☎055 248 07 78; www.terrazzamenoni.it; Piazza Ghiberti 11; meals €15-20; ⏲noon-2.30pm Mon-Sat) Luca Menoni's meat stall inside the Sant'Ambrogio covered market has been a favourite with locals since 1921 (his father first ran the business) and now the Florentine artisan has struck gold with a sassy self-service, zero-kilometre *risto macelleria* (butcher's eatery) above his market stall. Everything is homemade and ingredients are sourced fresh from the morning market.

★Il Teatro del Sale TUSCAN €€
(Map p53; ☎055 200 14 92; www.teatrodelsale.com; Via dei Macci 111r; brunch/dinner €20/30; ⏲noon-2.30pm & 7-11pm Tue-Fri, noon-3pm & 7-11pm Sat, noon-3pm Sun, closed Aug) Florentine chef Fabio Picchi is one of Florence's living treasures who steals the Sant'Ambrogio show with this eccentric, good-value,

PIZZA FIX

Santarpia (Map p53; ☎055 24 58 29; www.santarpia.biz; Largo Pietro Annigoni 9c; pizza €8.50-15; ⏲7.30pm-midnight Tue-Sun; 📶) Thin-crust Neapolitan pizza near Mercato di Sant'Ambrogio.

Gustapizza (Map p53; ☎055 28 50 68; www.facebook.com/GustapizzaFirenze; Via Maggio 46r; pizza €5-8; ⏲11.30am-3.30pm & 7-11.30pm Tue-Sun) Student favourite, Neapolitan-style, on the Oltrarno.

SimBIOsi (Map p53; ☎055 064 01 15; www.simbiosi.bio; Via de' Ginori 56r; pizza €6.50-11; ⏲noon-11pm; 📶) Hipster pizzeria cooking organic pizza, with craft beer and wine by small producers.

members-only club (everyone welcome; membership €7) inside an old theatre. He cooks up brunch and dinner, culminating at 9.30pm in a live performance of drama, music or comedy arranged by his wife, artistic director and comic actress Maria Cassi.

Dinners are hectic: grab a chair, serve yourself water, wine and antipasti, and wait for the chef to yell out what's about to be served before queuing at the glass hatch for your *primo* (first course) and *secondo* (second course). Note: this is the only Picchi restaurant to serve pasta! Dessert and coffee are laid out buffet-style just prior to the performance.

Enoteca Pinchiorri TUSCAN **€€€**
(Map p53; ☎055 2 63 11; www.enotecapinchiorri.com; Via Ghibellina 87r; 7-/8-course menu €250/275; ⏲7.30-10pm Tue-Sat, closed Aug) Niçoise chef Annie Féolde applies French techniques to her refined Tuscan cuisine and does it so well that this is the only restaurant in Tuscany to brandish three shiny Michelin stars. Imagine pigeon roasted in a cocoa-bean crust, with a salted-peanut emulsion and black-truffle sauce. The setting is a 16th-century *palazzo* hotel and the wine list is out of this world.

Oltrarno

★#Raw VEGAN **€**
(Map p53; ☎055 21 93 79; www.hashtagraw.it; Via Sant'Agostino 11r; meals €8-15; ⏲10am-6pm Tue-Fri, 11am-8pm Sat & Sun; 📶🌱) Should you desire a turmeric, ginger or aloe vera shot or a gently warmed, raw vegan burger served on a stylish slate-and-wood platter, innovative Raw hits the spot. Everything served here is freshly made and raw – to sensational effect. Herbs are grown in the biodynamic greenhouse of charismatic and hugely knowledgeable chef Caroline, a Swedish architect before moving to Florence.

★Il Santo Bevitore TUSCAN **€€**
(Map p56; ☎055 21 12 64; www.ilsantobevitore.com; Via di Santo Spirito 64-66r; meals €40; ⏲12.30-2.30pm & 7.30-11.30pm, closed Sun lunch & Aug) Reserve or arrive right on 7.30pm to snag the last table at this ever-popular address, an ode to stylish dining where gastronomes eat by candlelight in a vaulted, whitewashed, bottle-lined interior. The menu is a creative reinvention of seasonal classics: pumpkin gnocchi with hazelnuts, coffee and green-veined *blu di Capra* (goat cheese), *tagliatelle* with hare *ragù,* garlic cream and sweet Carmignano figs...

BEST GELATERIE

My Sugar (Map p53; ☎393 0696042; Via de' Ginori 49r; cones €2.50-4.50, tubs €2.50-5; ⏲1-11pm summer, to 8.30pm winter, closed Jan & Feb) Sensational artisan gelateria near Piazza San Marco.

Grom (Map p56; ☎055 21 61 58; www.grom.it; Via del Campanile 2; cones & tubs €2.60-5.50; ⏲10am-midnight Sun-Fri, to 1am Sat summer, 10.30am-10.30pm winter) Top-notch gelato, including outstanding chocolate, near the *duomo*.

Venchi (Map p56; ☎055 26 43 39; www.venchi.com; Via dei Calzaluoli 65; 2-/3-/4-scoops €3.20/4/5; ⏲10am-11pm Sun-Thu, to midnight Fri & Sat) Who can resist an entire wall flowing with melted chocolate?

★Gurdulù RISTORANTE **€€**
(Map p53; ☎055 28 22 23; www.gurdulu.com; Via delle Caldaie 12r; meals €40, tasting menu €55; ⏲7.30-11pm Tue-Sat, 12.30-2.30pm & 7.30-11pm Sun; 📶) Gourmet Gurdulù seduces fashionable Florentines with razor-sharp interior design, magnificent craft cocktails and seasonal market cuisine from young local chef Gabriele Andreoni. A hybrid drink-dine, this address is as much about noshing gourmet *aperitivi* snacks over expertly mixed cocktails (€12) or an expertly curated Tuscan wine flight (€25 for four wines) as it is about dining exceedingly well.

★Essenziale TUSCAN **€€€**
(Map p53; ☎333 7491973, 055 247 69 56; www.essenziale.me; Piazza di Cestello 3r; 6-/8-course tasting menu €65/80; ⏲7-10pm Tue-Sat; 📶) There's no finer showcase for modern Tuscan cuisine than this loft-style restaurant in a 19th-century warehouse. Preparing dishes at the kitchen bar in rolled-up shirt sleeves and navy butcher's apron is dazzling young chef Simone Cipriani. Order one of his tasting menus to sample the full range of his inventive, thoroughly modern cuisine inspired by classic Tuscan dishes.

Drinking & Nightlife

Florence's drinking scene covers all bases. Be it historical cafes, contemporary cafes with barista-curated specialist coffee, traditional *enoteche* (wine bars, which invariably make great eating addresses too), trendy bars with lavish *aperitivo* buffets, secret speakeasies or edgy cocktail or craft-beer bars, drinking is fun and varied. Nightlife, less extravagant, revolves around a handful of dance clubs.

Duomo & Piazza della Signoria

Mayday Club COCKTAIL BAR

(Map p56; ☎055 238 12 90; www.maydayclub.it; Via Dante Alighieri 16; cocktails €8-10; ⏲8pm-2am Tue-Sat) Strike up a conversation with passionate mixologist Marco Arduino at Mayday. Within seconds you'll be hooked on his mixers and astonishing infusions, all handmade using wholly Tuscan ingredients. Think artichoke- and thistle-infused vermouth, pancetta whisky and porcini liqueur. Marco's cocktail list is equally impressive – or tell him your favourite flavours and let yourself be surprised.

Amblé BAR

(Map p56; ☎055 26 85 28; www.amble.it; Piazzetta dei Del Bene 7a; ⏲10am-midnight Tue-Sat, from noon Sun) 'Fresh food and old furniture' is the catchy strapline of this cafe-bar hidden in an alleyway near Ponte Vecchio. Vintage furniture – all for sale – creates a shabby-chic vibe and the tiny terrace feels delightfully far from the madding crowd on summer evenings. From the river, follow Vicolo dell'Oro to Hotel Continentale, then turn left along the alley running parallel to the river.

Tosca & Nino CAFE

(Map p56; ☎055 493 34 68; www.toscanino.com; Piazza della Repubblica 1, La Rinascente; meals €25-35; ⏲9am-midnight Mon-Sat, from 10.30am Sun) 'Tasting Tuscany' is the driver behind the rooftop hybrid crowning central department store La Rinascente on people-busy Piazza della Repubblica. As much quality eatery as a fashionable place to drink: nip up here between boutiques to gloat with the birds over coffee, cocktails or wine on its rooftop terrace. Views of the *duomo* and Florentine hills beyond are predictably dreamy.

STREET ETIQUETTE

In a bid to keep things clean and pretty in Renaissance Florence, the city mayor passed a law in September 2018 banning al fresco eating at certain times on specific streets and squares in the historic centre – on Via de'Neri, Via della Ninna, Piazzale degli Uffizi and Piazza del Grano from noon to 3pm and 6pm to 10pm. The mayor also introduced stiff fines of up to €500 for those who dared disobey. In reality, however, street eating remains very much alive and well in town, with huge crowds happily gathering outside popular eateries at lunchtime to chow tripe-stuffed *panini* (sandwiches) and other Florentine street-food delights on the hop. To avoid the wrath of both the city mayor and city-proud Florentines, avoid littering and head for the riverbanks or a city park to dine alfresco.

Santa Maria Novella

★Fabbricato Viaggiatori BAR

(Map p53; ☎055 264 51 14; www.facebook.com/fabbricatoviaggiatori; Piazza del Stazione 50; ⏲8am-midnight) An experimental 'factory' of people, ideas, food, wine, cocktails and live music is the essence of this funky new hangout, at home in Palazzina Reale di Santa Maria Novella – the striking, white marble Rationalist building from the 1930s adjoining the central train station. Be it breakfast, daytime drinks or dining, DJ sets, wine tasting or late-night dancing, it's an upcoming hybrid to watch.

★Manifattura COCKTAIL BAR

(Map p56; ☎055 239 63 67; www.facebook.com/Manifattura-626623900875649; Piazza di San Pancrazio 1; ⏲6pm-1am Tue-Thu & Sun, to 2am Fri & Sat) 'Made in Italy' has never been such a pertinent buzzword in the city, hence this trendy cocktail bar – an unabashed celebration of Italian spirits and other drinks, both alcoholic and soft. Behind the bar, Fabiano Buffolini is one of Florence's finest mixologists, tapas-style small plates of traditional Tuscan dishes make wonderful pairings and the music is undeniably retro (think 1950s Italian).

Tenax CLUB

(☎393 9204279, 335 5235922; www.tenax.org; Via Pratese 46; admission varies; ⏲10pm-4am Thu-Sun Oct-Apr) The only club in Florence on the European club circuit, with great international guest DJs and wildly popular 'Nobody's Perfect' house parties on Saturday night; find the warehouse-style building out of town near Florence airport. Take bus 29 or 30 from Stazione di Santa Maria Novella.

SIMONA BOTTONE/SHUTTERSTOCK ©

Piazza della Signoria

San Lorenzo & San Marco

★PanicAle COCKTAIL BAR

(Map p53; ☎335 5473530; www.facebook.com/PanicAleFirenze; Via Panicale 7-9r; ⊙5.30pm-1am Mon-Wed & Sun, to 2am Thu-Sat) Still lovingly known as Lo Sverso (its original name) by many a Florentine socialite, this superstylish bar is a gem. In a part of town where hipster addresses are scarce, there's no finer spot for an expertly crafted cocktail mixed with homemade syrups (try the basil), craft beer on tap or home-brewed ginger ale. DJs spin tunes many a weekend.

★Buca 10 WINE BAR

(Map p53; ☎055 016 53 28; www.facebook.com/enotecabuca10; Via Fiesolana 10r; ⊙3.30pm-midnight Tue-Thu, to 2am Fri & Sat; 📶) 'Peace and Wine' is the alluring strapline of this contemporary *enoteca*, run with an arty passion and creativity by Francesca and Daniele. Tasty *taglieri* (tasting boards) accompany the excellent wine list, there is a guitar and *cajón* (Peruvian percussion instrument) lying around for anyone to tinkle on, and the modern space hosts occasional photography exhibitions, film screenings and other local happenings.

Bitter Bar COCKTAIL BAR

(Map p53; ☎340 5499258; www.bitterbarfirenze.it; Via di Mezzo 28r; ⊙9pm-2am Mon-Sat) The 1920s provide the sassy inspiration behind this speakeasy where ordering anything so mundane as a Sex on a Beach is simply not done. Mixologist Cristian Guitti experiments with plenty of unusual bitters, infusions and fresh ingredients to keep cocktail aficionados on their toes, while tasting notes on the tantalising menu – 'sweet smooth', 'fresh and delicate', 'for gin lovers' – pander to the less initiated.

Santa Croce

★Ditta Artigianale CAFE

(Map p53; ☎055 274 15 41; www.dittaartigianale.it; Via de' Neri 32r; ⊙8am-10pm Mon-Thu, to midnight Fri, 9am-midnight Sat, to 11pm Sun; 📶) With industrial decor and laid-back vibe, this ingenious coffee roastery is a perfect place to hang at any time of day. The creation of three-times Italian barista champion Francesco Sanapo, it's famed for its first-class coffee and outstanding gin cocktails. If you're yearning for a flat white, cold-brew tonic or cappuccino made with almond milk, come here.

★Locale COCKTAIL BAR

(Map p53; ☎055 906 71 88; www.localefirenze.it; Via delle Seggiole 12; ⊙7.30pm-2am) At home in a 13th- to 15th-century *palazzo*, this tucked-away drinking and dining space is designed to stun. From the exquisite craft cocktails (€20 to €30) mixed at the bar, to the beautifully presented modern Tuscan fare and awe-inspiring interior design – a theatrical fusion of original architectural features, period furnishings and contemporary vegetal wall gardens – Locale is a true feast for the eyes (and appetite).

Le Murate CAFE

(Caffè Letterario Firenze; Map p53; ☎055 234 68 72; www.lemurate.it; Piazza delle Murate; ⊙10.30am-1am Mon-Fri, from 4pm Sat & Sun;) This arty cafe-bar in Florence's former jail is where literati meet to talk, create and perform over coffee, drinks and light meals. The literary cafe hosts everything from readings and interviews with authors – Florentine, Italian and international – to film screenings, debates, live music and art exhibitions. Tables are built from recycled window frames and in summer everything spills outside into the brick courtyard.

Oltrarno

★ Santarosa Bistrot BAR

(Map p53; ☎055 230 90 57; www.facebook.com/santarosa.bistrot; Lungarno di Santarosa; ⊙8am-midnight;) The living is easy at this hipster garden-bistro-bar, snug against a chunk of ancient city wall in the flowery Santarosa gardens. Comfy cushioned sofas built from recycled wooden crates sit alfresco beneath trees; food is superb (meals €30); and mixologists behind the bar complement an excellent wine list curated by Enoteca Pitti Gola e Cantina with serious craft cocktails.

Spaghetti jazz soirées and other music events set the bar buzzing after dark. In warmer weather, grab a picnic hamper for two and enjoy an intimate lunch amid greenery.

★ Le Volpi e l'Uva WINE BAR

(Map p53; ☎055 239 81 32; www.levolpieluva.com; Piazza dei Rossi 1; ⊙11am-9pm Mon-Sat) This humble wine bar remains as appealing as the day it opened in 1992. Its food and wine pairings are first class – taste and buy boutique wines by small Italian producers, matched perfectly with cheeses, cold meats and the finest crostini in town; the warm, melt-in-your-mouth *lardo di cinta senese* (wafer-thin slices of aromatic of pork fat) is absolutely extraordinary.

There are wine-tasting classes too – or simply work your way through the impressive 50-odd different wines available by the glass (€4.50 to €9).

★ Mad Souls & Spirits COCKTAIL BAR

(Map p53; ☎055 627 16 21; www.facebook.com/madsoulsandspirits; Borgo San Frediano 38r; ⊙6pm-2am;) At this ubercool bar in San Frediano, cult alchemists Neri Fantechi and Julian Biondi woo a discerning crowd with their expertly crafted cocktails, served in a tiny aqua-green and red-brick space that

RADIOKAFKA/SHUTTERSTOCK ©

Mercato Centrale (p62)

couldn't be more spartan. A potted cactus decorates each scrubbed wood table and the humorous cocktail menu is the height of irreverence. Check the 'Daily Madness' blackboard for specials.

★Gosh COCKTAIL BAR
(Map p56; ☎055 046 90 48; www.facebook.com/goshfirenze; Via Santo Spirito 46r; ⏲7pm-midnight Tue-Thu, 6pm-2am Fri-Sun) Whimsical flamingo wallpaper, funky music, DJ sets and a subtle NYC vibe lures Florence's fashionable set to this buzzing cocktail bar across the river. Expect lots of fun variations of classic cocktails – blueberry mojitos, dozens of different Moscow mules and sensational basil-infused creations.

★Enoteca Pitti Gola e Cantina WINE BAR
(Map p53; ☎055 21 27 04; www.pittigolaecantina.com; Piazza dei Pitti 16; ⏲1pm-midnight Wed-Mon) Wine lovers won't do better than this serious wine bar opposite Palazzo Pitti, run with passion and humour by charismatic trio Edoardo, Manuele and Zeno – don't be surprised if they share a glass with you over wine talk. Floor-to-ceiling shelves of expertly curated, small-production Tuscan and Italian wines fill the tiny bar, and casual dining is around a handful of marble-topped tables. Look forward to excellent cured meats and pasta *fatta in casa* (housemade).

Shopping

Tacky mass-produced souvenirs (boxer shorts emblazoned with *David's* packet) are everywhere, not least at city market **Mercato Nuovo** (Map p56; Piazza del Mercato Nuovo; ⏲8.30am-7pm Mon-Sat), awash with cheap imported handbags and other leather goods. But for serious shoppers keen to delve into a city synonymous with artisanship since medieval times, there are ample addresses.

★Benheart FASHION & ACCESSORIES
(Map p56; www.benheart.it; Via dei Calzaivoli 78; ⏲10am-7.30pm) This flagship store of local superstar Ben, a Florentine-based fashion designer who set up the business with schoolmate Matteo after undergoing a heart transplant, is irresistible. The pair swore that if Ben survived, they'd go it alone – which they did, with huge success. For real-McCoy handcrafted leather designs – casual shoes, jackets and belts for men and women – there is no finer address.

LOCAL KNOWLEDGE

HISTORIC CAFES

Caffè Gilli (Map p56; ☎055 21 38 96; www.gilli.it; Piazza della Repubblica 39r; ⏲7.30am-1am) The most famous of the historic cafes on the city's old Roman forum, serving delectable cakes, fruit tartlets and *millefoglie* (vanilla or custard slice) since 1733.

Procacci (Map p56; ☎055 21 16 56; www.procacci1885.it; Via de' Tornabuoni 64r; ⏲10am-9pm Mon-Sat, 11am-8pm Sun, closed 3 weeks Aug) The last remaining bastion of genteel old Florence on Via de' Tornabuoni, this tiny cafe was born in 1885. Order bite-sized *panini tartufati* (truffle pâté rolls) and prosecco (sparkling wine).

Caffè Rivoire (Map p56; ☎055 21 44 12; www.rivoire.it; Piazza della Signoria 4; ⏲7am-midnight Tue-Sun summer, to 9pm winter) Golden oldie from 1872 with an unbeatable people-watching terrace and exquisite chocolate (sadly only available in winter).

★Officina Profumo-Farmaceutica di Santa Maria Novella GIFTS
(Map p56; ☎055 21 62 76; www.smnovella.it; Via della Scala 16; ⏲9am-8pm) In business since 1612, this exquisite perfumery-pharmacy began life when Santa Maria Novella's Dominican friars began to concoct cures and sweet-smelling unguents using medicinal herbs cultivated in the monastery garden. The shop, with an interior from 1848, sells fragrances, skincare products, ancient herbal remedies and preparations for everything from relief of heavy legs to improving skin elasticity, memory and mental energy.

★Lorenzo Villoresi PERFUME
(Map p53; ☎055 234 11 87; www.lorenzovilloresi.it; Via de' Bardi 14; ⏲10am-7pm Mon-Sat) Artisanal perfumes, bodycare products, scented candles and stones, essential oils and room fragrances crafted by Florentine perfumer Lorenzo Villoresi meld distinctively Tuscan elements such as laurel, olive, cypress and iris with essential oils and essences from around the world. His bespoke fragrances are highly sought after and visiting his elegant boutique, at home in his family's 15th-century *palazzo*, is quite an experience.

★Mio Concept HOMEWARES

(Map p56; ☎055 264 55 43; www.mio-concept.com; Via della Spada 34r; ⏰10am-1.30pm & 2.30-7.30pm Mon-Sat) Design objects for the home – made in Italy and many upcycled – as well as jewellery, bags and belts crafted from old bicycle tyres and inner tubes by Turinese designers Cingomma, and so on, cram this stylish boutique created by German globetrotter Antje. Don't miss the prints of iconic designs by Italian street artists Blub and Exit Enter, and street-sign artworks by Florence's **Clet** (Map p53; ☎339 2203607, 347 3387760; Via dell'Olmo 8r; ⏰hours vary).

★Luisa Via Roma FASHION & ACCESSORIES

(Map p56; ☎055 906 41 16; www.luisaviaroma.com; Via Roma 19-21r; ⏰10.30am-7.30pm Mon-Sat, from 11am Sun) The flagship outlet of this historic store (think: small 1930s boutique selling straw hats) turned luxury online retailer is a must for the fashion-forward. Eye-catching window displays woo with giant screens, while seasonal themes transform the interior maze of rooms into an exotic Garden of Eden. Shop here for lesser-known designers as well as popular luxury-fashion labels. Pre- or post-shop, hob-nob with the city's fashionista set over fair-trade coffee, organic cuisine and creative cold-press juices in Luisa's chic 1st-floor cafe-bar **Floret** (☎055 29 59 24; www.floret-bar.com; salads & bowls €12-16; 📶) 🌿.

★Street Doing VINTAGE

(Map p53; ☎055 538 13 34; www.streetdoingvintage.it; Via dei Servi 88r; ⏰10.30am-7.30pm Mon-Sat, from 2.30pm Sun) Vintage couture for men and women is what this extraordinary rabbit warren of a boutique – surely the city's largest collection of vintage – is about. Carefully curated garments and accessories are in excellent condition and feature all the top Italian designers: beaded 1950s Gucci clutch bags, floral 1960s Pucci dresses, Valentino shades from every decade.

PARKING IN FLORENCE

There is a strict Limited Traffic Zone (ZTL) in Florence's historic centre between 7.30am and 7.30pm Monday to Friday and 7.30am to 6pm Saturday for all nonresidents, monitored by cyclopean cameras positioned at all entry points. The exclusion also applies on Thursday, Friday and Saturday nights from 11pm to 3am from the first Sunday in April to the first Sunday in October. Motorists staying in hotels within the zone are allowed to drive to their hotel to drop off luggage, but must tell reception their car registration number and the time they were in no-cars-land (there's a two-hour window) so that the hotel can inform the authority and organise a permit. If you transgress, a fine of up to €200 will be sent to you (or the car-hire company you used). For more information see www.comune.fi.it.

There is free street parking around Piazzale Michelangelo and plenty of car parks costing around €3.80 per hour around town, including at Stazione di Santa Maria Novella, by Fortezza da Basso and in the Oltrarno beneath Piazzale di Porta Romana. Find a complete list of car parks on www.fipark.com.

ℹ Information

EMERGENCY

Police Station (Questura; ☎055 4 97 71, English-language service 055 497 72 68; http://questure.poliziadistato.it/it/Firenze; Via Zara 2; ⏰24hr, English-language service 9.30am-1pm Mon-Fri)

MEDICAL SERVICES

24-Hour Pharmacy (☎055 21 67 61; Stazione di Santa Maria Novella; ⏰24hr)

Dr Stephen Kerr: Medical Service (☎335 8361682, 055 28 80 55; www.dr-kerr.com; Piazza Mercato Nuovo 1; ⏰3-5pm Mon-Fri, or by appointment 9am-3pm Mon-Fri)

Hospital (Ospedale di Santa Maria Nuova; ☎055 6 93 81; www.asf.toscana.it; Piazza di Santa Maria Nuova 1; ⏰24hr)

TOURIST INFORMATION

Airport Tourist Office (☎055 31 58 74; www.firenzeturismo.it; Via del Termine 11, Florence Airport; ⏰9am-7pm Mon-Sat, to 2pm Sun)

Infopoint Bigallo (Map p56; ☎055 28 84 96; www.firenzeturismo.it; Piazza San Giovanni 1; ⏰9am-7pm Mon-Sat, to 2pm Sun)

Tourist Office (Map p56; ☎055 21 22 45; www.firenzeturismo.it; Piazza della Stazione 4; ⏰9am-7pm Mon-Sat, to 2pm Sun)

ℹ Getting There & Around

AIR

Florence Airport (Aeroporto Amerigo Vespucci; ☎055 306 18 30, 055 3 06 15; www.aeroporto.firenze.it; Via del Termine 11) is 5km northwest of the city centre and is served by both domestic and European flights.

BICYCLE

Florence by Bike (☎055 48 89 92; www.florencebybike.com; Via San Zanobi 54r; 1hr/5hr/1 day €3/9/12; ⏱9am-1pm & 3.30-7.30pm Mon-Sat, 10am-7pm Sun) Bike shop with rental (city, mountain, touring and road bikes), itinerary suggestions and tours (two-hour photography tours of the city by bike, and day trips to Chianti).

Florence Station Rental (☎055 045 07 05; www.florencestationrental.com; Via XXVII Aprile 37-41r; ⏱9.30am-7pm summer, to 5pm winter) Bike rental.

CAR & MOTORCYCLE

Florence is connected by the A1 northwards to Bologna and Milan, and southwards to Rome and Naples. The Autostrada del Mare (A11) links Florence with Pistoia, Lucca, Pisa and the coast, but most locals use the FI-PI-LI – a *superstrada* (dual carriageway, hence no tolls); look for blue signs saying FI-PI-LI (as in Firenze-Pisa-Livorno). Another dual carriageway, the S2, links Florence with Siena. The much more picturesque SS67 connects the city with Pisa to the west, and Forli and Ravenna to the east.

Within Florence, nonresident traffic is banned from the historic centre; parking is an absolute headache and best avoided.

PUBLIC TRANSPORT

Buses and electric minibuses run by public-transport company **ATAF** (www.ataf.net) serve the city. Most buses – including bus 13 to Piazzale Michelangelo – start/terminate at the ATAF bus stops opposite the southeastern exit of Stazione di Santa Maria Novella.

Buy tickets at the **ATAF ticketing window** (Map p53; ☎800 424500; www.ataf.net; Stazione di Santa Maria Novella, Piazza della Stazione; ⏱6.45am-8pm) inside the main ticket hall at Stazione di Santa Maria Novella, and at kiosks and tobacconists around town. Upon boarding, time stamp your ticket (punch on board) or risk an on-the-spot €50 fine.

Tickets, valid for 90 minutes (no return journeys), cost €1.50 from the window or ticket machines (€2.50 onboard or €1.80 via SMS with an Italian SIM card); children shorter than 1m travel for free. A 10-ticket carnet/monthly travel pass is €14/35.

TAXI

For a taxi, call 055 42 42 (www.4242.it) or 055 43 90 (www.4390.it), or use the IT Taxi smartphone app.

EASTERN TUSCANY

The eastern edge of Tuscany is beloved by both Italian and international film directors, who have immortalised its landscape, hilltop towns and oft-quirky characters in several critically acclaimed and visually splendid films.

Arezzo

☎0575 / POP 99,400

Arezzo may not be a Tuscan centrefold, but those parts of its historic centre that survived merciless WWII bombings are as compelling as any destination in the region – the city's central square is as beautiful as it appears in Roberto Benigni's classic film *La vita è bella* (Life is Beautiful; 1997).

Once an important Etruscan trading post, today the city is known for its churches, museums and fabulously sloping Piazza Grande, across which a huge antiques fair spills each month. Come dusk, Arentini (locals of Arezzo) spill along the length of shop-clad Corso Italia for the ritual late-afternoon *passeggiata* (stroll).

Sights

A combined ticket (adult/reduced €12/8) covers admission to Cappella Bacci, Museo Archeologico Nazionale, Museo di Casa Vasari and Museo Nazionale d'Arte Medievale e Moderna. It's valid for two days and can be purchased at each museum.

★Chiesa di Santa Maria della Pieve CHURCH

(Corso Italia 7; ⏱8am-12.30pm & 3-6.30pm) FREE This 12th-century church – Arezzo's oldest – has an exotic Romanesque arcaded facade adorned with carved columns, each individually decorated. Above the central doorway are 13th-century carved reliefs called *Cyclo dei Mesi* representing each month of the year. The plain interior's highlight – being restored at the **RICERCA Restoration Studio** (☎0575 2 86 70, 333 2851179; www.ricercarestauro.wordpress.com; Via Mazzini 1; by donation; ⏱by appointment) at the time of research – is Pietro Lorenzetti's polyptych *Madonna and Saints* (1320–24). Below the altar is a 14th-century silver bust reliquary of the city's patron saint, San Donato.

★Cappella Bacci CHURCH

(☎0575 35 27 27; www.pierodellafrancesca.it; Piazza San Francesco; adult/reduced €8/5; ⏱9am-6pm Mon-Fri, to 5.30pm Sat, 1-5.30pm Sun, extended hours summer) This chapel, in the apse of 14th-century **Basilica di San Francesco**, safeguards one of Italian art's greatest works: Piero della Francesca's fresco cycle of the *Legend of the True Cross*. Painted between 1452 and 1466, it relates the story of the cross on which Christ was crucified. Only 30 people are allowed in every half hour, making advance booking (by telephone or email) essential in high season.

★ Museo Archeologico Nazionale 'Gaio Cilnio Mecenate' MUSEUM
(Gaius Cilnius Maecenas Archeological Museum; ☎0575 2 08 82; www.facebook.com/archeologicoarezzo; Via Margaritone 10; adult/reduced €6/3; ⏰8.30am-7.30pm Mon-Sat) Overlooking the remains of a Roman amphitheatre that once seated up to 10,000 spectators, this museum – named after Gaius Maecenas (68–8 BC), a patron of the arts and trusted advisor to Roman emperor Augustus – exhibits Etruscan and Roman artefacts in a 14th-century convent building. The highlight is the *Cratere di Euphronios,* a 6th-century-BC Etruscan vase decorated with vivid scenes showing Hercules in battle.

Sleeping

Graziella Patio Hotel BOUTIQUE HOTEL €€
(☎0575 40 19 62; www.hotelpatio.it; Via Cavour 23; d €160-180, ste €210-285; ❄@📶) Each of the 10 rooms at this central hotel has decor inspired by Bruce Chatwin's travel books. Pink-kissed Arkady is the 'Australia room', Fillide exudes a distinctly Moroccan air and Cobra Verde is a green Amazon-inspired loft. Every room has a Macbook for guests to go online; wi-fi access on smartphones is pretty well nonexistent.

★ Villa Fontelunga BOUTIQUE HOTEL €€€
(☎0575 66 04 10; www.fontelunga.com; Via Cunicchio 5, Foiano della Chiana; d €240-410, villa per week €2730-4830; ⏰mid-Mar–Oct; P❄📶🏊) Gorgeous is the only word to use when describing this 19th-century villa in Foiano della Chiana, 35km southwest of Arezzo. Its nine rooms are the perfect balance of traditional Tuscan elegance and jet-set pizzazz.

Arezzo

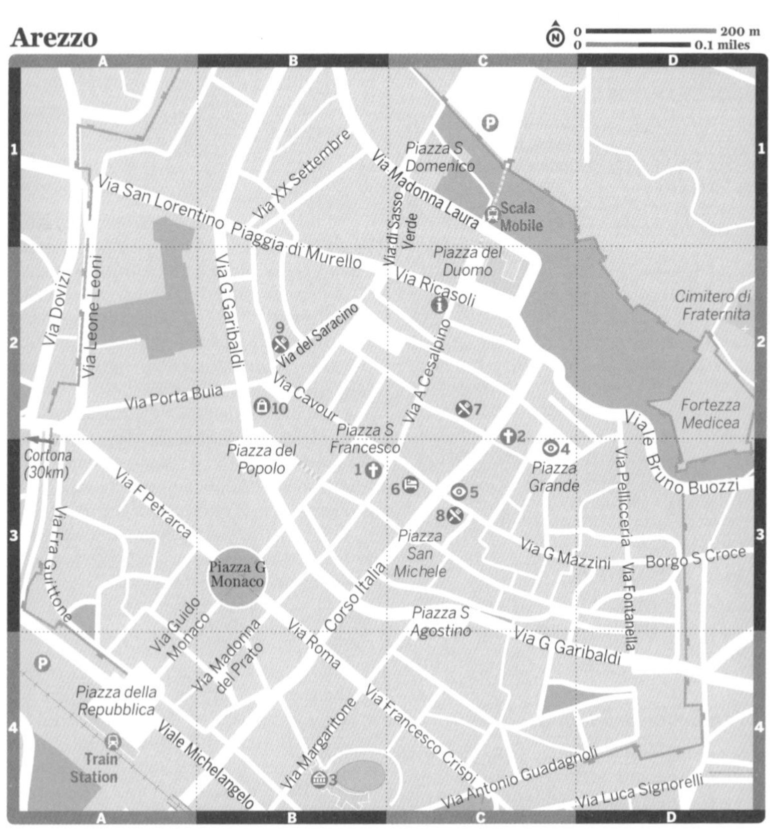

Facilities include a tennis court, stunning pool and mountain-bike use. Dinner (€39 including wine) is offered twice weekly.

Eating

L'Antica Bottega di Primo SANDWICHES **€**
(☎0575 04 01 24; www.facebook.com/Bottegadiprimo; Via Cavour 92; panini €2.50-4; ⏰7.30am-9pm Mon-Thu, to 11pm Fri-Sun; 📶) A delectable array of local cheese and cured meats awaits at this popular *alimentari* (grocery store), which fills fresh *panini* and focaccias to order and also sells delicious freshly baked biscuits and pastries. Eat in or take away.

★**Antica Osteria Agania** TUSCAN **€**
(☎0575 29 53 81; www.agania.com; Via Mazzini 10; meals €20; ⏰noon-3pm & 6-10.30pm Tue-Sun) Operated by the Ludovichi family since 1905, Agania serves the type of diehard traditional fare that remains the cornerstone of Tuscan dining. Specialities include sensational antipasti (with lots of vegetarian options), rustic soups, homemade pasta and *secondi* ranging from *lumache* (snails) to *grifi* (lambs' cheeks) with polenta, *baccalà* (cod) with chickpeas, and sausages with beans.

★**Aliciati** ITALIAN **€€**
(☎0575 2 72 41; www.aliciati.com; Via Bicchieraia 16-18; meals €38; ⏰12.30-2.30pm & 7.30-10pm Tue-Sun) Chef Giovanni Aliciati reimagines classic Italian dishes using top-quality ingredients and incorporating French and Spanish techniques and flavours. The refined results are as good to taste as they are to look at. The interior of the restaurant, which is near **Piazza Grande**, is equally impressive, with contemporary glass light fittings throwing golden light on stone walls.

LOCAL KNOWLEDGE

AREZZO MARKET TALK

A treasure trove of locally grown and produced food, **Mercato Logge del Grano** (☎0575 2 06 46; www.facebook.com/loggedelgrano; Piazzetta a delle Loggia del Grano; ⏰9am-2.30pm & 4.30-8pm Mon-Sat) is a superb organic market selling fresh meat, fruit and vegetables, olive oil, dried pasta and legumes, bread, wine and dairy products including milk and cheese. It's a sensational resource for self-caterers. Free tastings are offered every Saturday and also at special openings on the first Sunday of each month.

Arezzo

Sights
1 Cappella Bacci........B3
2 Chiesa di Santa Maria della Pieve........C2
3 Museo Archeologico Nazionale 'Gaio Cilnio Mecenate'........B4
4 Piazza Grande........C3
5 RICERCA Restoration Studio........C3

Sleeping
6 Graziella Patio Hotel........C3

Eating
7 Aliciati........C2
8 Antica Osteria Agania........C3
9 L'Antica Bottega di Primo........B2

Shopping
10 Mercato Logge del Grano........B2

Information

Tourist Office (Centro Accoglienza Turistica; ☎0575 40 19 45; www.arezzointuscany.it; Piazza della Libertà; ⏰10am-4pm)

Casentino Valley

Parco Nazionale delle Foreste Casentinesi, Monte Falterona e Campigna

One of three national parks in Tuscany, the Parco Nazionale delle Foreste Casentinesi, Monte Falterona e Campigna (Casentino Forests, Mount Falterona and Campigna National Park) straddles the Tuscany-Emilia-Romagna border and protects scenic stretches of the Apennines and Italy's largest forest and woodlands.

One of the highest peaks, **Monte Falterona** (1654m), marks the source of the river Arno. The park is home to a rich assortment of wildlife, including nearly 100 bird species. Nine self-guided nature trails criss-cross the park: most popular is the 4.5km uphill hike (4½ hours return) from San Benedetto in Alpe to the **Acquacheta Waterfall**, made famous by Dante's *Divine Comedy*.

The major settlement in the park is **Badia Prátaglia**, a small village in the Alpe di Serra mountain range, near the border with Emilia-Romagna.

Accommodation is scant. Pilgrims can stay in basic quarters at the Camaldoli and Verna monasteries (p46). There is an excellent pool-clad **sleeping option** (☎0575 55 62

04; www.itrebaroni.it; Via di Camaldoli 52, Moggiona; s €65-75, d €75-85, ste €110-280; ⏲Easter-Oct; P 📶 🏊) with grandiose views in the tiny hamlet of Moggiona, on the park's southwestern fringe; or use nearby Poppi as a base.

Information

National Park Tourist Office (☎0575 50 30 29; www.parcoforestecasentinesi.it; Via Guido Brocchi 7, Pratovecchio; ⏲9am-1pm Mon-Fri)

Poppi

☎0575 / POP 6150

Seeming to float in the clouds above the Arno plain, Poppi Alta (the historic upper section of the town) is crowned by the commanding presence of the Castello dei Conti Guidi (p47). The kiosk in the piazza outside the castle is the social hub during the summer; at other times locals tend to socialise in Ponte a Poppi (the lower town).

Sleeping & Eating

★**Borgo Corsignano** AGRITURISMO €€
(☎0575 50 02 94; www.borgocorsignano.it; Via Corsignano, Corsignano; d/q from €150/300; P @ 📶 🏊) In a *borgo* (medieval hamlet) once home to Camaldoli monks, this gorgeous country hotel is the Casentino's finest accommodation option. A 5km drive from Poppi, it has a mix of self-catering apartments and houses spread lavishly among 13 old stone properties. Voluptuous sculptures collected by the art-loving owners pepper the vast grounds, and sweeping mountain views are magnificent.

L'Antica Cantina TUSCAN €€
(☎0575 52 98 44; www.anticacantina.com; Via Lapucci 2; meals €38; ⏲noon-2.30pm & 8-11pm Tue-Sat, noon-3pm Sun Feb-Dec; 📶) This old-fashioned dining experience cooks up traditional Tuscan beneath an atmospheric vaulted ceiling. Find it on a steep side street off Via Cesare Battisti in Poppi Alta.

Sansepolcro

☎0575 / POP 15,900

This hidden gem is a town that truly deserves that description. Dating from the year 1000, Sansepolcro (called 'Borgo' by locals) reached its current size in the 15th century and was walled in the 16th century. Its historic centre is littered with *palazzi* and churches squirrelling away Renaissance works of art or bejewelled with exquisite terracotta Andrea della Robbia medallions. Spend a day wandering from dimly lit church to church, following in the footsteps of Sansepolcro's greatest son, Renaissance artist Piero della Francesca.

Sights

★**Museo Civico** MUSEUM
(☎0575 73 22 18; www.museocivicosansepolcro.it; Via Niccolò Aggiunti 65; adult/reduced €10/8.50, with Casa di Piero della Francesca €11/9.50; ⏲10am-1.30pm & 2.30-6.40pm mid-Jun–mid-Sep, reduced hours est of year) The town's flagship museum is home to a collection that includes two Piero della Francesca masterpieces – *Resurrection* (1458–74) and the *Madonna della Misericordia* (Madonna of Mercy; 1445–56) polyptych – as well as fresco fragments portraying *San Ludovico* (Saint Ludovic; 1460) and *San Giuliano* (Saint Julian; 1460). Also of note are works from the studio of Andrea della Robbia, including a beautiful tondo (circular sculpture) known as the *Virgin and Child with Manetti Coat of Arms* (1503).

Sleeping & Eating

★**Dolce Rosa** PENSION €
(☎366 3973527; www.dolcerosa.it; Via Niccolò Aggiunti 74; s/d €45/60; ❄) It's rare to find budget accommodation that is well located, super-clean and extremely comfortable, but that's what's on offer at this excellent *pensione* near the Museo Civico. Host Rodolfo looks after his guests well, providing kettles and mini-fridges stocked with complimentary water and soft drinks. No breakfast, but at these prices, who's quibbling?

★**Pasticceria Chieli** CAFE €
(☎0575 74 20 26; www.pasticceriachieli.it; Viale Vittorio Veneto 35; ⏲6am-8pm Tue-Fri, to 8.30pm Sat, 6.30am-1.30pm Sun; ❄) Just outside the historic town walls, Sansepolcro's best cafe bustles at all times of the day. It's a go-to destination whether you're after a morning coffee and pastry, a lunchtime *panino*, a cake in the afternoon or an *aperitivo* (predinner drink). Staff are friendly and there's plenty of seating too.

★**Ristorante Al Coccio** TUSCAN €€
(☎0575 74 14 68; www.alcoccio.com; Via Niccolò Aggiunti 83; meals €40; ⏲12.30-2.30pm & 7.30-9.30pm Wed-Mon; ❄) 🌿 Sisters Sara and Loide Battistelli head the kitchen and dining room of this elegant restaurant, which serves organic produce and plenty of gluten-free choices. The locally sourced beef is a highlight – order a *tagliata* of dry-aged Chianina or a carpaccio topped with shaved

black truffle and *parmigiano reggiano*. Great desserts too.

Information

Tourist Office (☎ 0575 74 05 36; www.valtiberinaintoscana.it; Via Giacomo Matteotti 8; ⏰10am-1pm & 2.30-6.30pm mid-Mar–Oct, shorter hours winter; 📶)

Cortona

☎ 0575 / POP 22,100

Rooms with a view are the rule rather than the exception in this spectacularly sited hilltop town. At the beginning of the 15th century Fra' Angelico lived and worked here, and fellow artists Luca Signorelli and Pietro da Cortona were both born within the walls – all three are represented in the Museo Diocesano's small but sensational collection. Large chunks of *Under the Tuscan Sun*, the 2003 film of the book by Frances Mayes, were shot here and the town has been a popular tourist destination ever since.

Sights

★Museo Diocesano di Arte Sacra MUSEUM

(☎ 0575 6 28 30; Piazza del Duomo 1; adult/reduced €5/3; ⏰10am-6.30pm Apr-Oct, 11am-4pm Tue-Fri, 10am-5pm Sat & Sun Nov-Mar) Highlights of this small museum in the decommissioned 16th-century Chiesa del Gesù include a number of works by Pietro Lorenzetti, a *Madonna and Child* (c 1336) by Niccolò di Segna and two beautiful works by Fra' Angelico: *Annunciation* (1436) and *Madonna with Child and Saints* (c 1438). Upstairs, the Sala Signorelli is home to two paintings by the Cortona-born artist, including *Lamentation Over the Dead Christ* (1502).

Museo dell'Accademia Etrusca e della Città di Cortona MUSEUM

(MAEC; ☎ 0575 63 04 15; www.cortonamaec.org; Piazza Signorelli 9; adult/reduced €10/7; ⏰10am-7pm Apr-Oct, to 5pm Tue-Sun Nov-Mar) Spread over five floors in the 13th-century **Palazzo Casali**, the collection here includes substantial local Etruscan and Roman finds, Renaissance globes, 18th-century decorative arts and an eclectic array of paintings. The Etruscan collection is the highlight – don't miss the extraordinary hanging bronze lamp on the 2nd floor. Paintings to look for include Luca Signorelli's sinister *Madonna with Child and Saint Protectors of Cortona* (1512) and Gino Severini's exquisite *Maternità* (1916).

Sleeping

Villa Marsili HOTEL €€

(☎ 0575 60 52 52; www.villamarsili.net; Viale Cesare Battisti 13; s €75-85, d €110-220; ⏰Apr-Nov; P ❄ 📶) Service is the hallmark at this attractive villa wedged against the city walls and a short walk downhill from Cortona centre. Guests rave about the helpful staff, lavish breakfast buffet and early-evening *aperitivo* served in the garden. Pricier suites have hot tubs and wonderful views across the Val di Chiana to Lago Trasimeno. Advance, non-refundable rates are considerably reduced.

Monastero di Cortona Hotel & Spa LUXURY HOTEL €€€

(☎ 0575 178 58 39; www.monasterodicortona.com; Via del Salvatore; r €195-300, ste €350; P ❄ 📶 🏊) The monks who once called this monastery home wouldn't recognise their quarters these days, as a 2018 makeover transformed the heritage building into an alluring luxury hotel. Rooms are elegant and well equipped, and facilities include an atmospheric spa with indoor pool, garden with plunge pool, and bar with 17th-century frescoes.

Eating

Taverna Pane e Vino TUSCAN €

(☎ 0575 63 10 10; www.pane-vino.it; Piazza Signorelli 27; bruschette €4, cheese & meat boards €7-13; ⏰noon-11pm Tue-Sun) Simple seasonal dishes are the trademark of this vaulted cellar, a hotspot with local bon vivants who come to indulge in their pick of Tuscan and Italian wines in the company of bruschette and generous platters of cheese and cured meats.

La Bucaccia TUSCAN €€

(☎ 0575 60 60 39; www.labucaccia.it; Via Ghibellina 17; meals €38; ⏰12.30-2.30pm & 7-10.30pm Tue-Sun) Occupying the medieval stable of a Renaissance *palazzo*, Cortona's best-regarded restaurant has close-set tables where diners enjoy refined versions of Cortonese specialities – beef, game and handmade pasta feature on the menu. Owner Romano Magi ripens his own cheeses and starting or ending your meal with a cheese course is recommended. There's an excellent wine list too. Reservations essential.

Information

Tourist Office (☎ 0575 63 72 23; www.comunedicortona.it/turismo-e-cultura/info-cortona; Piazza Signorelli 9; ⏰10am-7pm Apr-Oct, 9am-1pm Mon-Thu, 10am-5pm Fri-Sun Nov-Mar)

Siena & Southern Tuscany

Siena's architecture soars, while its vibrant streets are lined with tempting boutiques and restaurants. Picturesque Chianti provides the grapes for its namesake wines.

Siena

☎0577 / POP 53,900

Siena is a city where the architecture soars, as do the souls of many of its visitors. Effectively a giant, open-air museum celebrating the Gothic, Siena has spiritual and secular monuments that have retained both their medieval forms and their extraordinary art collections, providing the visitor with plenty to marvel at. The city's historic *contrade* (districts) are marvellous too, being as close-knit and colourful today as they were in the 17th century when their world-famous horse race, the Palio, was inaugurated. And within each *contrada* lie vibrant streets populated with artisanal boutiques, sweet-smelling *pasticcerie* (pastry shops) and tempting restaurants. It's a feast for the senses and an essential stop on every Tuscan itinerary.

Sights

★Piazza del Campo PIAZZA

Popularly known as 'Il Campo', this sloping piazza has been Siena's social centre since being staked out by the ruling Consiglio dei Nove (Council of Nine) in the mid-12th century. Built on the site of a Roman marketplace, its paving is divided into nine sectors representing the members of the *consiglio,* and these days acts as a carpet on which young locals meet and relax. The cafes around its perimeter are the most popular coffee and *aperitivo* (predinner drinks) spots in town.

★Complesso Museale di Santa Maria della Scala MUSEUM

(☎0577 28 63 00; www.santamariadellascala.com; Piazza Duomo 2; adult/reduced €9/7; ⊙10am-7pm Fri-Wed, to 10pm Thu mid-Mar–mid-Oct, to 5pm Mon, Wed & Fri, to 8pm Thu, to 7pm Sat & Sun mid-Oct–mid-Mar) Built as a hospice for pilgrims travelling the Via Francigena, this huge complex opposite the *duomo* (cathedral) dates from the 13th century. Its highlight is the upstairs **Pellegrinaio** (Pilgrim's Hall), featuring vivid 15th-century frescoes by Lorenzo di Pietro (aka Vecchietta), Priamo della Quercia and Domenico di Bartolo. All laud the good works of the hospital and its patrons; the most evocative is di Bartolo's *Il governo degli infermi* (Caring for the Sick; 1440–41), which depicts many activities that occurred here.

Palazzo Pubblico HISTORIC BUILDING

(Palazzo Comunale; Piazza del Campo) Built to demonstrate the enormous wealth, proud independence and secular nature of Siena, this 14th-century Gothic masterpiece is the visual focal point of the Campo, itself the true heart of the city. Architecturally clever (notice how its concave facade mirrors the opposing convex curve) it has always housed the city's administration and been used as a cultural venue. Its distinctive bell tower, the **Torre del Mangia** (☎0577 29 26 15; ticket@comune.siena.it; adult/family €10/25; ⏲10am-6.15pm Mar–mid-Oct, to 3.15pm mid-Oct–Feb), provides magnificent views for those who brave the steep climb to the top.

★Museo Civico MUSEUM

(Civic Museum; ☎0577 29 26 15; Palazzo Pubblico, Piazza del Campo 1; adult/reduced €10/9, with Torre del Mangia €15, with Torre del Mangia & Complesso Museale di Santa Maria della Scala €20; ⏲10am-6.15pm mid-Mar–Oct, to 5.15pm Nov–mid-Mar) Entered via the Palazzo Pubblico's **Cortile del Podestà** (Courtyard of the Chief Magistrate), this wonderful museum showcases rooms richly frescoed by artists of the Sienese school. Commissioned by the city's governing body rather than by the Church, some of the frescoes depict secular subjects – highly unusual at the time. The highlights are two huge frescoes: Ambrogio Lorenzetti's *Allegories of Good and Bad Government* (c 1338–40) and Simone Martini's celebrated *Maestà* (Virgin Mary in Majesty; 1315).

★Duomo CATHEDRAL

(Cattedrale di Santa Maria Assunta; ☎0577 28 63 00; www.operaduomo.siena.it; Piazza Duomo; Mar-Oct €5, Nov-Feb free, when floor displayed €8; ⏲10.30am-6.30pm Mon-Sat & 1.30-5.30pm Sun Mar-Oct, 10.30am-5pm Mon-Sat & 1.30-5pm Sun Nov-Feb) Consecrated on the former site of a Roman temple in 1179 and constructed over the 13th and 14th centuries, Siena's majestic *duomo* showcases the talents of many great medieval and Renaissance architects and artists: Giovanni Pisano designed the intricate white, green and red marble facade; Nicola Pisano carved the elaborate pulpit; Pinturicchio painted the frescoes in the extraordinary Libreria Piccolomini; and Michelangelo, Donatello and Gian Lorenzo Bernini all produced sculptures.

To enjoy spectacular bird's-eye views, buy a ticket for the Porta del Cielo (Gate of Heaven) escorted tour up, into and around the building's roof and dome. Tour groups are capped at 18 participants and depart at fixed times throughout the day – purchase your ticket from the office in the Complesso Museale di Santa Maria della Scala. Arrive at the meeting point at least five minutes before your allocated tour time.

★Libreria Piccolomini LIBRARY

(Piccolomini Library; ☎0577 28 63 00; www.operaduomo.siena.it; Piazza Duomo; €2; ⏲10.30am-6.30pm Mon-Sat & 1.30-5.30pm Sun Mar-Oct, 10.30am-5pm Mon-Sat & 1.30-5pm Sun Nov-Feb) Cardinal Francesco Todeschini Piccolomini, archbishop of Siena (later Pope Pius III), commissioned the building and decoration of this hall off the north aisle of the *duomo* in 1492 to house the books of his uncle, Enea Silvio Piccolomini (Pope Pius II). Come here not to see the books (only a series of huge choral tomes remains on display), but to enjoy the vividly coloured narrative frescoes (1503–08) by Pinturicchio (Bernardino di Betto), which depict events in the life of Pius II.

★Pinacoteca Nazionale GALLERY

(☎0577 28 11 61; www.pinacotecanazionale.siena.it; Via San Pietro 29; adult/reduced €8/2, free 1st Sun of month Oct-Mar; ⏲8.15am-7.15pm Tue-Sat, 9am-1pm Sun & Mon) Siena's recently renovated art gallery, housed in 14th-century

DON'T MISS

IL PALIO

Dating from the Middle Ages, this spectacular annual event includes a series of colourful pageants and a wild horse race in Piazza del Campo on 2 July and 16 August. Ten of Siena's 17 *contrade* (town districts) compete for the coveted *palio* (silk banner). Each *contrada* has its own traditions, symbol and colours, plus its own church and *palio* museum.

From about 5pm on race days, representatives from each *contrada* parade in historical costume, all bearing their individual banners. For scarcely one exhilarating minute, the 10 horses and their bareback riders tear three times around a temporarily constructed dirt racetrack with a speed and violence that makes spectators' hair stand on end.

The race is held at 7.45pm in July and 7pm in August. Join the crowds in the centre of the Campo at least four hours before the start if you want a place on the rails, but be aware that once there you won't be able to leave for toilet or drink breaks until the race has finished. Alternatively, the cafes in the Campo sell places on their terraces; these cost between €280 and €400 per ticket. The tourist office can supply information about how to book tickets; this should be done up to one year in advance.

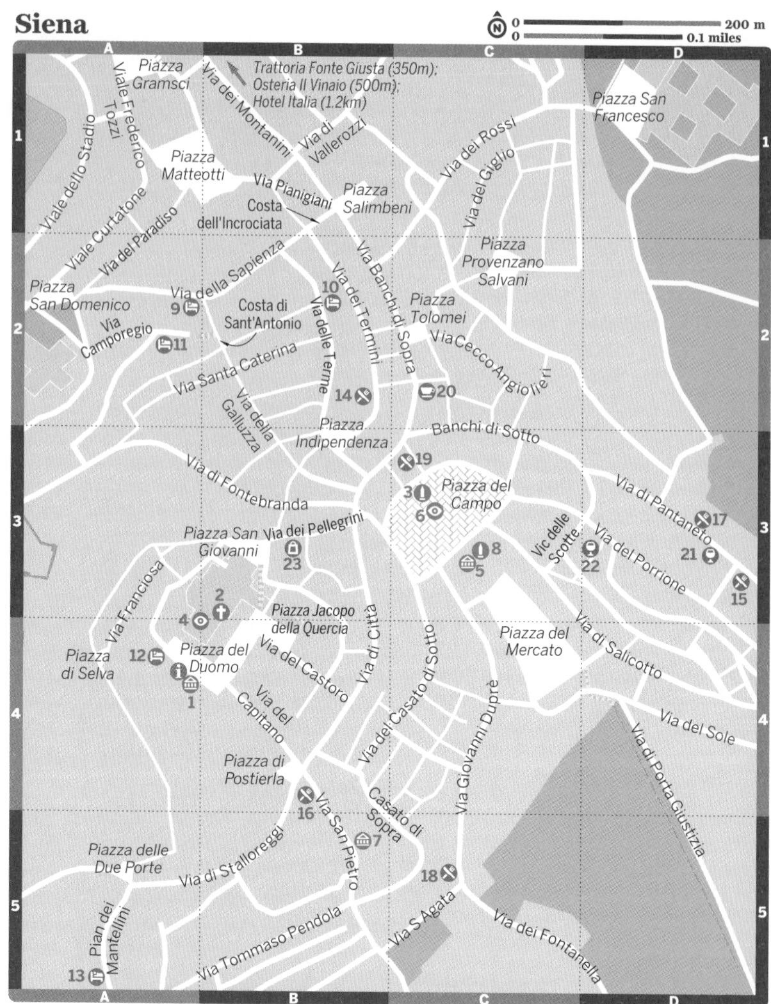

Palazzo Buonsignori since 1932, is home to an extraordinary collection of Gothic masterpieces from the Sienese school. These include works by Guido da Siena, Duccio (di Buoninsegna), Simone Martini, Niccolò di Segna, Lippo Memmi, Ambrogio and Pietro Lorenzetti, Bartolo di Fredi, Taddeo di Bartolo and Sano di Pietro.

Tours

Associazione Centro Guide CULTURAL
(AGT; ☎0577 4 32 73; www.guidesiena.it/en) One of three official local guides' associations. Operates two-hour tours to the Complesso Museale di Santa Maria della Scala and the Museo Civico from 3pm every Monday, Friday and Saturday between mid-April and October (adult/child under 11 €25/free). This departs from outside the tourist office (p79) in the Santa Maria della Scala complex. Other tours are detailed on the website.

Centro Guide Turistiche Siena e Provincia CULTURAL
(☎0577 4 32 73; www.guidesiena.it) Accredited guides offer guaranteed daily departures of a two-hour 'Classic Siena' Walking Tour (adult/child seven to 12/child under seven

Siena

Sights

1	Complesso Museale di Santa Maria della Scala	A4
2	Duomo	B3
3	Fonte Gaia	C3
4	Libreria Piccolomini	A4
5	Museo Civico	C3
	Palazzo Pubblico	(see 5)
6	Piazza del Campo	C3
7	Pinacoteca Nazionale	B5
8	Torre del Mangia	C3

Sleeping

9	Albergo Bernini	A2
10	Antica Residenza Cicogna	B2
11	Hotel Alma Domus	A2
12	Ostello Casa delle Balie	A4
13	Pensione Palazzo Ravizza	A5

Eating

14	Enoteca I Terzi	B2
15	La Prosciutteria	D3
16	La Vecchia Latteria	B4
17	Lievito M@dre	D3
18	Osteria La Taverna di San Giuseppe	C5
19	Te Ke Voi?	C3

Drinking & Nightlife

20	Bar Pasticcerie Nannini	C2
21	Bottega Roots	D3
22	UnTUBO	D3

Shopping

23	Il Magnifico	B3

€20/10/free) at 11am between April and October. This features key historical and cultural landmarks and includes entrance to the duomo or Santa Maria della Scala. Tours in English and Italian depart from outside the tourist information office in Santa Maria della Scala (p74).

Sleeping

Siena is blessed with a wide variety of accommodation types. Note that prices skyrocket and minimum-stay requirements are implemented during the Palio (p75).

Ostello Casa delle Balie HOSTEL €
(☎347 6137678; ostellosms@operalaboratori.com; Vicolo di San Girolamo 2; dm €18; ⏲reception 11am-4.30pm & 7-9.15pm; ❄@📶) Siena's historic centre sorely lacks backpacker accommodation, so we were thrilled when this hostel just off Piazza Duomo opened in 2017. Though primarily catering to pilgrims walking the Via Francigena, it also welcomes others – book in advance. Rooms have bunk beds and small lockers (sheets and blankets provided); hot showers cost €0.50. Laundry facilities (charged), but no kitchen or lounge.

Albergo Bernini PENSION €
(☎0577 28 90 47; www.albergobernini.com; Via della Sapienza 15; d €100, without bathroom €80; 📶) The tiny terrace alone might prompt you to stay at this welcoming, family-run hotel – it sports grandstand views across to the *duomo* and is a captivating spot for a drink at sunset. The 10 bedrooms are traditional affairs and only a couple have air-con. Cash payment only.

Hotel Alma Domus HOTEL €
(☎0577 4 41 77; www.hotelalmadomus.it; Via Camporegio 37; s €46-55, d €72-140; ❄@📶) Your chance to sleep in a convent: Alma Domus is owned by the church and is still home to several Dominican nuns. The economy rooms, although comfortable, are styled very simply and aren't as soundproofed as many would like. But the superior ones are lovely, with stylish decor and modern fittings; many have minibalconies with uninterrupted *duomo* views.

Antica Residenza Cicogna B&B €€
(☎0577 28 56 13; www.anticaresidenzacicogna.it; Via delle Terme 76; s/d/ste €90/110/150; ❄@📶) You'll get a true feel for Siena's history in this 13th-century *palazzo* close to the Campo. Tiled floors, ornate lights and painted ceilings meet tones of yellow ochre and (suitably) burnt sienna. All of the rooms are charming, but we were particularly taken with the Stanza dei Paesaggi, which is named after the frescoed landscapes that decorate it.

Hotel Italia HOTEL €€
(☎0577 4 42 48; www.hotelitalia-siena.it; Viale Cavour 67; s €70-122, d €140-175; P❄@📶) Close to both the train station and the busy shopping and eating strip of Via Camollia, this well-priced modern hotel offers a range of accommodation, including worn but comfortable standard rooms and swish, newly built executive rooms. Parking costs €10 per night, the breakfast buffet is generous and guests can use the swimming pool at a nearby hotel in the same group.

★ **Pensione Palazzo Ravizza** BOUTIQUE HOTEL €€€
(☎0577 28 04 62; www.palazzoravizza.it; Pian dei Mantellini 34; r €170-330; P ❄ ☜) Occupying a Renaissance-era *palazzo* located in a quiet but convenient corner of Siena, the Ravizza offers rooms perfectly melding traditional decor and modern amenities; the best face the large rear garden, which has a panoramic terrace. The breakfast buffet is generous, on-site parking is free if you book directly with the hotel and room rates are remarkably reasonable (especially in low season).

Eating

Among the many traditional local dishes served in Siena are *panzanella* (summer salad of soaked bread, basil, onion and tomatoes), *ribollita* (a rich vegetable, bean and bread soup), *pappardelle alla lepre* (ribbon pasta with hare), *panforte* (a rich cake of almonds, honey and candied fruit) and *ricciarelli* (sugar-dusted chewy almond biscuits). Keep an eye out for dishes featuring the region's signature *cinta senese* (indigenous Tuscan pig).

★ **La Vecchia Latteria** GELATO €
(☎0577 05 76 38; www.facebook.com/GelateriaYogurteriaLaVecchiaLatteria; Via San Pietro 10; gelato €2-4.50; ⏲noon-11pm, to 8pm winter) Sauntering through Siena's historic centre is always more fun with a gelato in hand. Just ask one of the many locals who are regular customers at this *gelateria artigianale* (maker of handmade gelato) near the Pinacoteca Nazionale. Using quality produce, owners Fabio and Francesco concoct and serve fruity fresh or decadently creamy iced treats – choose from gelato or frozen yoghurt.

Te Ke Voi? FAST FOOD €
(☎0577 4 01 39; Vicolo di San Pietro 4; burgers €10-14, pizza €7-10, focaccias €4.50-5.50; ⏲noon-3.30pm & 6.30pm-midnight Mon-Thu, noon-1am Fri & Sat, noon-midnight Sun; ✍) The name means 'Whaddya want?' and the answer is simple – cheap and tasty food prepared fast and served in pleasant surrounds. Beloved of local students, it serves focaccias, salads, risottos, pastas, pizzas and burgers (including veggie options). The *pasta cresciuta* (fried pasta) goes down a treat with a cold beer or glass of wine. Order at the counter.

Osteria Il Vinaio TUSCAN €
(☎0577 4 96 15; Via Camollia 167; dishes €6.50-13; ⏲10am-10pm Mon-Sat) Wine bars are thin on the ground in Siena, so it's not surprising that Bobbe and Davide's neighbourhood *osteria* (casual tavern) is so popular. Join the multigenerational local regulars for a bowl of pasta or your choice from the generous antipasto display, washed down with a glass or two of eminently quaffable house wine.

Enoteca I Terzi TUSCAN €€
(☎0577 4 43 29; www.enotecaiterzi.it; Via dei Termini 7; meals €42; ⏲12.30-3pm & 7.30-11pm Mon-Sat) Close to the Campo but off the well-beaten tourist trail, this *enoteca* (wine bar) is located in a vaulted medieval building but has a contemporary feel. It's popular with sophisticated locals, who linger over working lunches, *aperitivo* sessions and slow-paced dinners featuring Tuscan *salumi* (cured meats), delicate handmade pasta, grilled meats and wonderful wines (many available by the glass).

Trattoria Fonte Giusta TUSCAN €€
(☎0577 4 05 06; Via Camollia 102; meals €30; ⏲7-11pm Mon-Fri, noon-2.30pm & 7-11pm Sat & Sun; ✍) The huge slabs of Chianina beef displayed in a refrigerated cabinet in the window signals one of the specialities at this family-run trattoria on the historic Via Francigena pilgrimage route through town. Other draws include hand-made pasta, flavourful seasonal antipasti, house-made gelato and home-style cakes. The owners also run the highly regarded **Fonte Giusta Cooking School**

PICNIC PERFECT

Prosciutto is the focus at **La Prosciutteria** (☎0328 541 43 25; www.laprosciutteria.com; cnr Via Pantaneto & Vicolo Magalotti; panini €4-7, tasting boards from €10; ⏲11.30am-3.30pm & 5.30pm-midnight Mon-Thu, 11.30am-12.30am Sat; ☜), served in *panini* (sandwiches) or on a *taglieri* (tasting plate); cheese is an optional extra. Order to take away – the Orto de' Pecci is close by – or claim one of the tables on the street and enjoy a glass of wine (€2.50) too. An *aperitivo* costs €5.

Near the Campo, popular bakery-cum-cafe **Lievito M@dre** (☎0577 151 54 51; www.facebook.com/LievitoMadreSiena; Via di Pantaneto 59; meal deal €6.90, pizzas €6-12; ⏲7.30am-11pm Sun-Thu, to midnight Fi & Sat; ☜✍) is a recommended address for filled *panini* and pizza slices to take away (or eat in).

DON'T MISS

SWEET SIENA

Lorenzo Rossi is Siena's best baker, and his *panforte, ricciarelli* and *cavallucci* are a weekly purchase for most local households. Try them at **Il Magnifico** (☎0577 28 11 06; www.ilmagnifico.siena.it; Via dei Pellegrini 27; ⊙7.30am-7.30pm Mon-Sat), his bakery and shop behind the *duomo*, and you'll understand why.

(Fonte Giusta Scuola di Cucina; ☎0577 4 05 06; www.scuoladicucinafontegiusta.com; Via Camollia 78; per person €100; ⊙4.30-7pm).

★Osteria La Taverna di San Giuseppe TUSCAN €€€
(☎0577 4 22 86; www.tavernasangiuseppe.it; Via Dupré 132; meals €49; ⊙noon-2.30pm & 7-10pm Mon-Sat) Any restaurant specialising in beef, truffles and porcini mushrooms attracts our immediate attention, but not all deliver on their promise. Fortunately, this one does. A favoured venue for locals celebrating important occasions, it offers excellent food, an impressive wine list with plenty of local, regional and international choices, a convivial traditional atmosphere and efficient service.

Drinking & Nightlife

Via Camollia and Via di Pantaneto are Siena's major bar and coffee strips. Though atmospheric, the bars lining the Campo are expensive if you sit at a table – consider yourself warned.

Bar Pasticcerie Nannini CAFE
(☎0577 23 60 09; www.pasticcerienannini.it/en; Via Banchi di Sopra 24; ⊙7.30am-10pm Mon-Thu, to 11pm Fri & Sat, to 10pm Sun) Established in 1886, Nannini's good coffee and location near the Campo ensure that it remains a local favourite. It's a great place to sample Sienese treats including *cantuccini* (crunchy, almond-studded biscuits), *cavallucci* (chewy biscuits flavoured with aniseed and other spices), *ricciarelli* (chewy, sugar-dusted almond biscuits), *panforte* (dense spiced cake with almonds and candied fruit) and *panpepato* (*panforte* with the addition of pepper and hazelnuts).

Bottega Roots BAR
(☎0577 89 24 82; www.facebook.com/bottegarootssiena; Via di Pantaneto 58; ⊙10.30am-2am; 📶) Located in Siena's student quarter, this bar stages live-music acts in a vaulted interior with a mezzanine area. Artisan beer is the tipple of choice. Check its Facebook page for the performance schedule.

UnTUBO CLUB
(☎0577 27 13 12; www.untubo.it; Vicolo del Luparello 2; cover charge varies; ⊙6.30pm-3am Tue-Sat) Live jazz acts regularly take the stage on Thursday and Friday nights at this intimate club near the Campo, which is popular with students and the city's boho set. Check the website for a full events program – blues, pop and rock acts drop in for occasional gigs too. Note that winter hours are often reduced.

Information

Tourist Office (☎0577 28 05 51; www.terresiena.it; Piazza Duomo 2, Santa Maria della Scala; ⊙10am-6pm mid-Mar–Oct, to 4.30pm Nov–mid-Mar)

Getting There & Around

CAR & MOTORCYCLE

To drive between Siena and Florence, take the Siena–Florence autostrada or the more scenic SR222.

There's a ZTL (Zona a Traffico Limitato; Limited Traffic Zone) in Siena's historic centre, although visitors can often drop off luggage at their hotel; ask reception to report your licence number in advance, or risk a hefty fine.

There are large car parks operated by **Siena Parcheggi** (☎0577 22 87 11; www.sienaparcheggi.com) at the Stadio Comunale and around the Fortezza Medicea, both just north of Piazza San Domenico (the website is a useful resource). Hotly contested free street parking (look for white lines) is available in Viale Vittorio Veneto on the Fortezza Medicea's southern edge. The paid car parks at San Francesco and Santa Caterina (aka Fontebranda) each have a free *scala mobile* (escalator) going up into the centre.

Most car parks charge €2 per hour between 7am and 8pm.

Chianti

The vineyards in this picturesque part of Tuscany produce the grapes used in namesake Chianti and Chianti Classico: world-famous reds sold under the Gallo Nero (Black Cockerel/Rooster) trademark. It's a landscape where you'll encounter historic olive groves, honey-coloured stone farmhouses, dense forests, graceful Romanesque

SIMONA BOTTONE/SHUTTERSTOCK ©

Montefioralle

pievi (rural churches), handsome Renaissance villas and imposing stone castles built in the Middle Ages by Florentine and Sienese warlords.

Though now part of the province of Siena, the southern section of Chianti (Chianti Senese) was once the stronghold of the Lega del Chianti, a military and administrative alliance within the city-state of Florence that comprised Castellina, Gaiole and Radda. Chianti's northern part sits in the province of Florence (Chianti Fiorentino) and is a popular day trip from that city. The major wine and administrative centres are Greve in Chianti, Castellina in Chianti and Radda in Chianti.

For regional information, including festivals and special events, see www.wechianti.com and www.chianti.com.

Greve in Chianti

☎0558 / POP 13,800

The main town in the Chianti Fiorentino, Greve is a hub of the local wine industry. It's not picturesque (most of the architecture is modern and unattractive), but it does boast an attractive, historic central square and a few notable businesses. The annual wine fair **Expo del Chianti Classico** is held in early September – if visiting at this time, book accommodation here and throughout the region well in advance.

Sights & Activities

Montefioralle VILLAGE

Medieval Montefioralle crowns a rise just east of Greve, and can be accessed via a 2km walking path from the town centre (head up Via San Francesco, off Via Roma). Surrounded by olive groves and vineyards, the village was home to Amerigo Vespucci (1415–1512), an explorer who followed Columbus' route to America. Vespucci wrote so excitedly about the New World that he inspired cartographer Martin Waldseemüller (creator of the 1507 *Universalis Cosmographia*) to name the new continent in his honour.

Enoteca Falorni WINE

(☎0558 54 64 04; www.enotecafalorni.it; Piazza delle Cantine 2-6; tastings by glass €0.60-30; ⌚10.30am-7.30pm Apr-May, to 8pm Jun-Sep, 10am-7pm Thu-Mon Oct-Mar, closed 3 weeks Jan) A perfect place to let your palate limber up before visiting individual wineries, this *enoteca* stocks more than 1000 wines and offers 100 for tasting, including a huge array of Chianti Classico, IGTs and other Tuscan favourites. Leave your credit card as a guarantee or buy a non-refundable prepaid wine card (€5 to €100) to test your tipples of choice.

Castello di Verrazzano WINE

(☎0558 5 42 43; www.verrazzano.com; Via Citille, Greti; tours €21-68; ⌚9.30am-6pm Mon-Sat, 10am-1pm & 3-6.30pm Sun) This hilltop castle 3km north of Greve was once home to Giovanni da Verrazzano (1485–1528), who explored the North American coast and is commemorated in New York by the Verrazzano-Narrows Bridge. Today it presides over a 225-hectare wine estate offering a wide range of tours.

Sleeping

Antico Pastificio Ulisse Mariotti APARTMENT €
(339 8485564; www.anticopastificio.com; Via dell'Arco 13; s/d €53/62, apt from €84;) In central Greve, two buildings of this former pasta factory have been converted into neat double rooms and basic self-catering apartments sleeping up to 10 guests. It offers swimming pool, table tennis, children's playground, shady grassed garden, BBQ area and a washing machine for guest use (€2 per load). Wi-fi (charged) is in common areas only. No breakfast; two-night minimum stay.

★ **Borgo del Cabreo** AGRITURISMO €€€
(347 1174065, 0553 98 50 32; www.borgodelcabreo.it; Via Montefioralle Case Sparse 9; d €260-280, q villa €400; P) Manager Michele works hard to ensure that guests enjoy their stay at this boutique *agriturismo* owned by the Tenuta di Nozzole winery, offering an efficient check-in, pouring a complimentary *aperitivo* on arrival and organising everything from restaurant bookings to bicycle hire. Rooms are classically elegant and extremely comfortable; facilities include a fabulous pool terrace overlooking the estate's olive groves.

Eating

Bistro Falorni DELI €
(0558 5 30 29; www.falorni.it; Piazza Giacomo Matteotti 71; taglieri €7-9, panini €4-5, lasagne €6; 10am-7pm;) Italians do fast food differently, and what a wonderful difference it is. Greve's famous *macelleria* (butcher) and gourmet-provision shop operates this cafeteria attached to the *macelleria*, and it's popular with both locals and tourists. You can choose from the range of *taglieri* (tasting boards), *panini* and meat or vegetable lasagnes on offer, and enjoy a glass of wine (€4) too.

La Castellana TUSCAN €€
(0558 5 31 34; www.ristorantelacastellana.it; Via di Montefioralle 2, Montefioralle; meals €40; 12.30-2pm & 7.30-9.30pm Tue-Sun summer, hours vary winter) Located in a hamlet 2km above Greve, this well-regarded trattoria has six indoor tables and a hillside terrace overlooking cypresses, olive trees and vines. The home-style Tuscan cooking is wonderful – highlights include handmade ravioli stuffed with mushrooms and truffles, and succulent slices of rosemary-studded beef – and the wine list features many Chianti highlights.

Information

Tourist Office (0558 54 62 99, 0558 5 36 06; www.helloflorence.net; Piazza Matteotti 11; 10.30am-1.30pm late Mar–mid-Oct, to 6.30pm Easter-Aug) Located in Greve's main square.

CYCLING CHIANTI

Exploring Chianti by bicycle is a true highlight. The Greve in Chianti tourist office can supply information about local cycling routes, and the town is home to the well-regarded **Discovery Chianti** (328 6124658; www.discoverychianti.com; Via I Maggio 32; Mar-Oct), which runs guided cycling tours. It's also possible to rent bicycles from **Ramuzzi** (055 85 30 37; www.ramuzzi.com; Via Italo Stecchi 23; mountain or hybrid bike per day/week €20/130, e-bike/scooter per day €35/€65; 9am-1pm & 3-7pm Mon-Fri, 9am-1pm Sat) in Greve's town centre.

A number of companies (including Discovery Chianti) offer guided cycling tours leaving from Florence:

Florence by Bike (0554 8 89 92; www.florencebybike.it; Chianti guided bike tour adult/reduced €83/75; daily Mar-Oct)

I Bike Italy (342 9352395; www.ibikeitaly.com; 2-day Chianti guided bike tour road bike/e-bike €450/550; Mon, Wed & Fri mid-Mar–Oct)

We Bike Tuscany (USA 1-800-850-6832; www.webiketuscany.com; prices on application)

Getting There & Around

Greve is on the Via Chiantigiana (SR222). Find parking in the underground carpark next to Enoteca Falorni on the main road through town (€2/1 per 1st/subsequent hours 8am-8pm, €1/0.50 8pm-8am) or in the two-level, open-air car park on Via Luca Chini, on the opposite side of the main road to Piazza Matteotti, which is free on the top level. On Fridays, don't park overnight in the paid spaces in Piazza Matteotti – your car will be towed away to make room for Saturday market stalls.

Badia a Passignano

Chianti doesn't get much more atmospheric than Badia a Passignano, a Benedictine Vallombrosan abbey set amid vineyards run by the legendary Antinori dynasty. Head here to visit the historic church and abbey buildings, admire the views over the vineyards, and taste wines in the Antinori *enoteca* or in one of a number of good eateries located here.

Sights & Activities

Chiesa di San Michele Arcangelo CHURCH
(Abbey of Passignano; Via di Passignano; 10am-noon & 3-5pm Mon-Wed, Fri & Sat, 3-5pm Sun) An 11th-century church on this site was destroyed in the 13th century and replaced by this structure, which was subsequently heavily altered over the centuries. Dedicated to St Michael the Archangel (look for the 12th-century statue of him slaying a dragon next to the high altar), it is home to frescoes and paintings of varying quality – the best are by Domenico Cresti (known as 'Il Passignano') on the side walls of the transept.

Abbazia di San Michele Arcangelo a Passignano MONASTERY
(English 0558 07 23 41, Italian 0558 07 11 71; Via di Passignano; by donation; tours by reservation) The four Vallombrosan monks who call this medieval abbey home open their quarters to visitors on regular guided tours. The highlight is the refectory, which was remodelled in the 15th century and is presided over by Domenico Ghirlandaio's utterly marvellous, recently restored 1476 fresco *The Last Supper*. The tours also visit the monastery's garden cloister and historic kitchen. It's best to book in advance, as tour times can vary.

La Bottega di Badia a Passignano WINE
(0558 07 12 78; www.osteriadipassignano.com; Via di Passignano 33; 10am-7.30pm Mon-Sat) Taste or purchase Antinori wine in this *enoteca* beside the prestigious Osteria di Passignano restaurant. A tasting of three wines by the glass will cost between €20 and €50, and there is a variety of guided tours of the cellars and vineyards on offer – check the website for details. Wines by the glass cost between €6 and €23.

Sleeping & Eating

Torre di Badia B&B €€
(0550 16 41 60; www.torredibadia.com; Via Passignano 22; r €110-180;) Offering five comfortable rooms, this B&B in a recently restored medieval tower on the Badia di Passignano estate is a good choice for those wanting to explore the local area. In winter, the open fire and honesty bar in the lounge make for a welcoming retreat; in summer the garden terrace overlooking the Antinori vineyard beckons.

Fattoria di Rignana AGRITURISMO €€
(0558 5 20 65; www.rignana.it; Via di Rignana 15, Rignana; d from €95; Apr-Nov; P@) The historic *fattoria* (farmhouse) of this wine estate has its very own chapel and bell tower, which reveal themselves after you brave a long, rutted access road. You'll also find glorious views, a large swimming pool and a nearby eatery. Sleep in rustic en suite rooms in the *fattoria*. Find it 4km from Badia a Passignano.

★ **L'Antica Scuderia** TUSCAN €€
(0558 07 16 23, 335 8252669; www.ristorolanticascuderia.com; Via di Passignano 17; meals €45, pizza €12-20; 12.30-2.30pm & 7.30-10.30pm Wed-Mon;) The large terrace at this restaurant overlooks one of the Antinori vineyards and is perfect for summer dining. In winter, the elegant dining room comes into its own. Lunch features antipasti, pastas and traditional grilled meats, while dinner sees plenty of pizza-oven action. Kids love the playground set; adults love the fact that it keeps the kids occupied. There's a huge wine list.

Osteria di Passignano ITALIAN €€€
(055 807 12 78; www.osteriadipassignano.com; Via di Passignano 33; meals €85, tasting menus €90, wine pairing €140; 12.15-2.15pm & 7.30-10pm Mon-Sat; P) This elegant

ELENA ODAREEVA/SHUTTERSTOCK ©

Chiesa di San Michele Arcangelo

Michelin-starred eatery in the centre of Badia a Passignano has long been one of Tuscany's best-loved dining destinations. Intricate, Tuscan-inspired dishes fly the local-produce flag and the wine list is mightily impressive, with Antinori offerings aplenty. Vegetarians are well catered for, with a dedicated tasting menu available.

Getting There & Away

The easiest road access is via Strada di Badia off the SP94.

Radda in Chianti

0577 / POP 1580

The age-old streets in pretty Radda in Chianti fan out from its central square, where the heraldic shields of the 16th-century Palazzo del Podestà add a touch of drama to the scene. A historic wine town, it's the home of the Consorzio di Chianti Classico and is an appealing albeit low-key base for visits to some classic Tuscan vineyards, including those surrounding the historic hilltop hamlet of Volpaia, approximately 7km north of town.

Sights

Casa Chianti Classico MUSEUM

(0577 73 81 87; www.chianticlassico.com; Monastery of Santa Maria al Prato, Circonvallazione Santa Maria 18; self-guided tour €7; tours & tastings 11am-7pm Tue-Sat, to 5pm Sun mid-Mar–Oct) FREE Occupying an 18th-century convent complex attached to a 10th-century church, this facility is operated by the Consorzio di Chianti Classico and pays homage to the region's favourite product. Self-guided tours of the **Wine Museum** on the 1st floor introduce the terroir and history of the denomination and include an enjoyable multimedia quiz in which participants test their newly acquired oenological knowledge by analysing a glass of local wine (included in tour price).

The complex also has a tasting room off the main cloister (glass of wine €5 to €8), and a bistro (p84) incorporating a downstairs *enoteca* with a lovely terrace overlooking vineyards – perfect for a leisurely lunch or late-afternoon glass of wine. To find it, head downhill from Radda's main piazza.

Sleeping & Eating

Palazzo Leopoldo HOTEL €€

(0577 73 56 05; www.palazzoleopoldo.it; Via Roma 33; s/d/ste from €120/135/240; P) Like the idea of staying in a luxury hotel in an elegant 15th-century building but fear your budget won't stretch that far? This meticulously presented hotel may well be the answer. Well-equipped rooms and suites are located in the main building and an annexe; many have valley views. It has an indoor pool, outdoor hot tubs and a restaurant (meals €36).

Bistro Casa Chianti Classico TUSCAN €
(☎0577 73 81 87; www.chianticlassico.com; Monastery of Santa Maria al Prato, Circonvallazione Santa Maria 18; meals €23; ⌚noon-5pm Tue-Sun mid-Mar–Oct) Offering a seasonally driven menu and boasting (of course) a wonderful wine list, this bistro in the Chianti complex seats diners in the former kitchen and cloisters of an 18th-century convent, as well as in a downstairs *enoteca* with a terrace overlooking an adjoining vineyard. Try the signature *pici del convento* (pasta with confit tomato, almonds, olives and herbs).

Information

Tourist Office (☎0577 73 84 94; www.facebook.com/proradda; Piazza del Castello 2; ⌚10am-1pm Mon-Sat; 📶)

Getting There & Away

Radda is linked with Siena by the SP102 and with Castellina in Chianti by the SR429.

Panzano in Chianti

☎0558

Put on the tourist map by extrovert local butcher Dario Cecchini, this hilltop town on the Via Chiantigiana is a convenient eating stop for carnivores driving between Florence and Siena, who will enjoy eating at one of Cecchini's popular restaurants.

Located 10km south of Greve in Chianti, Panzano is known throughout Italy as the location of **L'Antica Macelleria Cecchini** (☎0558 5 20 20; www.dariocecchini.com; Via XX Luglio 11; ⌚9am-4pm), a butcher's shop owned and run by Dario Cecchini. This Tuscan celebrity has carved out a niche for himself as a poetry-spouting guardian of the *bistecca* (steak) and other Tuscan meaty treats, and he operates three eateries (p21) clustered around the *macelleria*.

Getting There & Away

Panzano in Chianti is on the SR222 from Florence to Siena.

Val d'Orcia

The picturesque agricultural valley of Val d'Orcia is a Unesco World Heritage site, as is the historic centre of the town of Pienza on its northeastern edge. The valley's distinctive landscape features flat chalk plains, out of which rise almost conical hills topped with fortified settlements and magnificent abbeys that were once important staging points on the Via Francigena.

For information about places, activities and events in the Val d'Orcia see www.parcodellavaldorcia.com.

Montalcino

☎0577 / POP 5920

Known globally as the home of one of the world's great wines, Brunello di Montalcino, the attractive hilltop town of Montalcino has a remarkable number of *enoteche* lining its medieval streets and is surrounded by hugely picturesque vineyards. There's history to explore too: the town's efforts to hold out against Florence even after Siena had fallen earned it the title 'the Republic of Siena in Montalcino', and there are many well-preserved medieval buildings within the historic city walls.

Sights & Activities

To save a couple of euros for your wine fund, purchase a combined ticket (adult/reduced €6/4.50) for entry to the **Fortezza's ramparts** (☎0577 84 92 11; Piazzale Fortezza; courtyard free, ramparts adult/reduced €4/2; ⌚9am-8pm Apr-Oct, 10am-6pm Nov-Mar) and the Museo Civico e Diocesano d'Arte Sacra. These are available from the tourist office.

Museo Civico e Diocesano d'Arte Sacra MUSEUM
(☎0577 84 60 14; www.facebook.com/museocivicoediocesanoearcheologicamontalcino; Via Ricasoli 31; adult/reduced €4.50/3; ⌚10am-1pm & 2-5.40pm Tue-Sun Sep-Mar, 10am-1pm & 2-5.50pm Apr-Oct) Occupying the former convent of the neighbouring **Chiesa di Sant'Agostino**, this collection of religious art from the town and surrounding region includes a triptych by Duccio and a *Madonna and Child* by Simone Martini. Other artists represented include the Lorenzetti brothers, Giovanni di Paolo and Sano di Pietro.

Enoteca La Fortezza WINE
(☎0577 84 92 11; www.enotecalafortezza.com; Piazzale Fortezza; ⌚9am-8pm, 10am-6pm in winter) The *enoteca* in Montalcino's medieval fortress offers a range of paid tastings, stocks a huge range of wine for sale and will ship overseas. Start with a tasting of three/five Brunellos (€14/20) and then consider graduating to two/three/five Riserva and Gran Selezioni vintages (€20/30/40).

Sleeping

Hotel Vecchia Oliviera HOTEL **€€**

(0577 84 60 28; www.vecchiaoliviera.com; Via Landi 1; r €145-180;) Chandeliers, polished wooden floors and rugs lend this converted oil mill a refined, albeit slightly worn, air. Of the 11 rooms on offer, opt for one in the superior category as these have great views (room 9 is best). The pool is in an attractive garden setting and the terrace has wrap-around views. Breakfast is disappointing.

Albergo Il Giglio HOTEL **€€**

(0577 84 81 67; www.gigliohotel.com; Via Soccorso Saloni 5; s/d €95/150;) There's a real old-world feel at this family-run place, something enhanced by the traditional Tuscan fireplace in the lounge and the brass bedsteads and arched ceilings in the 12 comfortable rooms. The views from upstairs windows are captivating – try to score room 1, which has its own panoramic terrace.

Eating

Trattoria L'Angolo TUSCAN **€**

(0577 84 80 17; Via Ricasoli 9; meals €22; noon-3pm Wed-Mon Sep-Jun, noon-3pm & 7-11pm Wed-Mon Jul & Aug) We thought about keeping shtum about this place (everyone loves to keep a secret or two), but it seemed selfish not to share our love for its pasta dishes. Be it vegetarian (ravioli stuffed with ricotta and truffles) or carnivorous (*pappardelle* with wild-boar sauce), the handmade *primi* (first courses) here are uniformly excellent. *Secondi* aren't as impressive.

★ **Re di Macchia** TUSCAN **€€**

(0577 84 61 16; redimacchia@alice.it; Via Soccorso Saloni 21; meals €35, set menus €27; noon-2pm & 7-9pm Fri-Wed;) Husband-and-wife team Antonio and Roberta run this relaxed eatery in the centre of town with great aplomb. Roberta's cooking is much more sophisticated than the Tuscan average but retains the usual laudable focus on local, seasonal produce. Antonio's excellent and affordable wine list is one of the best in town. The four-course set menus (one vegetarian) offer excellent value.

Information

Tourist Office (0577 84 93 31; www.prolocomontalcino.com; Costa del Municipio 1; 10am-1pm & 2-5.40pm, closed Mon winter) Just off the main square, this office can supply free copies of the *Consorzio del Vino Brunello*

LOCAL KNOWLEDGE

RURAL RETREATS

Motor just a few kilometres away from towns to uncover these absolutely exquisite rural retreats – perfect bases for exploring the Val d'Orcia.

La Bandita (333 4046704; www.la-bandita.com; Podere La Bandita, Località La Foce; r €250-550, self-contained ste €550; Apr-early Nov;) Sophisticated urban style melds with stupendous scenery at this rural retreat in one of the most stunning sections of the Val d'Orcia. Owned and operated by a former NYC music executive and his travel-writer wife (non–Lonely Planet, we hasten to add), it offers spacious rooms, amenities galore (we love the Ortigia toiletries), communal dinners (set menu €45 per person) and personalised service.

Foresteria Podere Brizio (0577 04 10 72; www.poderebrizio.it; Località Podere Brizio; r €230-255; closed Dec-Easter;) A huge amount of thought has gone into the design and construction of this splendid hotel on a wine estate 8km southwest of Montalcino, near Tavernelle. Rates are relatively restrained considering comfort and amenity levels in the spacious rooms and the wide array of facilities (huge swimming pool, restaurant, tennis court, spa).

Il Borgo (0577 87 77 00; www.castellobanfiilborgo.com; Castello Banfi, Poggio alle Mura, off SP117; r €450-1000, ste €700-1500; late Mar-late Nov;) Most of the 14 rooms on offer at Banfi's flagship Tuscan wine estate, wrapped around imposing medieval Castello di Poggio alla Mura, command wonderful views of vineyards and majestic Monte Amiata. Facilities include a heated pool, two formal restaurants and a pool bar serving drinks and light meals. Guests can use complimentary e-bikes to follow cycle routes through the vineyards.

di Montalcino map of wineries and also books cellar-door visits and winery accommodation.

Getting There & Away

To reach Montalcino from Siena, take the SS2 (Via Cassia); after Buonconvento, turn off onto the SP45. There's plenty of parking around the *fortezza* and in Via Pietro Strozzi (€1.50 per hour, 8am to 8pm).

Pienza

0578 / POP 2080

Once a sleepy hamlet, pretty Pienza was transformed when, in 1459, Pope Pius II began turning his home village into an ideal Renaissance town. The result is magnificent – the church, papal palace, town hall and accompanying buildings in and around Piazza Pio II went up in just three years and haven't been remodelled since. In 1996 Unesco added the town's historic centre to its World Heritage list, citing the revolutionary vision of urban space. On weekends, Pienza draws big crowds; come midweek if you possibly can.

Sights

★Museo Diocesano MUSEUM

See p30

Piazza Pio II PIAZZA

Stand in this magnificent square and spin 360 degrees. You've just taken in an overview of Pienza's major monuments. Gems of the Renaissance constructed in a mere three years between 1459 and 1462, they're arranged according to the urban design of Bernardo Rossellino, who applied the principles of Renaissance town planning devised by his mentor, Leon Battista Alberti.

★Duomo CATHEDRAL

(Concattedrale di Santa Maria Assunta; Piazza Pio II; 7.30am-1pm & 2-7pm) Pienza's *duomo* was built on the site of the Romanesque Chiesa di Santa Maria, of which little remains. The Renaissance church with its handsome travertine facade was commissioned by Pius II, who was so proud of the building that he issued a papal bull in 1462 forbidding any changes to it. The interior is a strange mix of Gothic and Renaissance styles and contains a superb marble tabernacle by Rossellino housing a relic of St Andrew the Apostle, Pienza's patron saint.

Sleeping

★La Bellavita B&B €€

(391 4392068; www.labellavitapienza.it; Via della Chiochina 1; r €90-140; closed Christmas;) Host Elisabetta goes out of her way to make guests feel at home in her cute four-room B&B. It can be hard to find – enter through the arch next to 81 Corso il Rossellino – but once you've arrived you'll be charmed by the clean and comfortable rooms, panoramic terrace and cute attic where a delicious buffet breakfast is served.

★La Bandita Townhouse BOUTIQUE HOTEL €€€

(0578 74 90 05; www.la-bandita.com/townhouse; Corso il Rossellino 111; r €350-€595; mid-Mar–early Jan; @) Aiming to provide their guests with a taste of Tuscan village life and Pienza with a world-class boutique hotel, the American owners of this boutique hotel purchased and renovated a Renaissance-era convent close to Piazza Pio – the result is both sensitive and supremely stylish. Facilities include a communal lounge with an honesty bar and a restaurant with a garden terrace.

Eating & Drinking

Osteria Sette di Vino TUSCAN €

(0578 74 90 92; Piazza di Spagna 1; snacks €3.50-7.50; noon-2.30pm & 7.30-10pm Thu-Tue) Known for its *zuppa di pane e fagioli* (bread and white-bean soup), bruschette, crostini and range of local *pecorino* (sheep's

Piazza Pio II and Duomo
FRANK BACH/SHUTTERSTOCK

milk cheese), this simple place has a clutch of tables inside and a scattering outside – book ahead.

Townhouse Caffè ITALIAN €€
(☎0578 74 90 05; www.la-bandita.com/townhouse/the-restaurant; Via San Andrea 8; meals €40; ⊙noon-2.30pm Tue-Sun, 7.30-10pm daily mid-Mar–early Jan;) The menu at this chic eatery is pared back in more ways than one: there are around four choices per course, presentation is minimalist and the emphasis is on the quality of the produce rather than clever culinary tricks – bravo! In summer, guests dine in an atmospheric medieval courtyard; in winter, the action moves into a two-room space with open kitchen.

★**Idyllium** BAR
(☎0578 74 81 76; www.facebook.com/idylliumbar; Via Gozzante 67; ⊙11am-2am summer, reduced hours rest of year) Located underneath Palazzo Piccolomini and accessed via the staircase between the palace and the *duomo,* this hybrid cafe and cocktail bar in the former palace stables has a terrace with wonderful views over the Val d'Orcia and towards Monte Amiata. Owners Bledar Ndoci and Federico Fioravanti learned their mixology art in Milan and definitely make the best cocktails in town.

Information

Tourist Office (☎0578 74 99 05; info.turismo@comune.pienza.si.it; Corso il Rossellino 30; ⊙10.30am-1.30pm & 2.30-6pm Wed-Mon mid-Mar–Oct, 10am-1pm & 2-5pm Sat & Sun Nov–mid-Mar)

Getting There & Around

On summer weekends finding a parking space in Pienza can be a real challenge as the car park near the centre (€1.50/5 per one/four hours) fills quickly. There is a limited number of free parking spaces on Via Circonvallazione below the *duomo,* but these are hotly contested.

Monticchiello

☎0578

Pretty as a picture, the medieval village of Monticchiello crowns a hill 10km south of Pienza. It makes a tranquil and convenient base when exploring the Val d'Orcia.

Sleeping & Eating

Ristorante Daria TUSCAN €€
See p30

★**La Casa di Adelina** B&B €
(☎0578 75 51 67; www.lacasadiadelina.eu; Piazza San Martino 3; d €95-120, 2-bed apt €125-200; ⊙closed mid-Nov–mid-Dec & mid-Jan–Feb;) Laden with art and atmosphere, this place has friendly hosts, a communal lounge with a wood stove (a joy in winter) and three comfortable rustic-chic rooms. The owners also have two apartments and one room in a newly renovated tower house, and a third stand-alone apartment with all the mod-cons that's perfect for an extended stay (when discounts apply).

Breakfast is provided for guests staying in rooms, but not for those in apartments.

La Guardiola TUSCAN €
(☎331 8800443; www.laguardiolawinefood.it; Viale Marino Cappelli 1; taglieri €12-14, crostini €7-10; ⊙9am-11pm Mon-Thu, to midnight Fri-Sun;) The pretty terrace at this wine bar next to the historic gate is a popular spot for lunch, a *merende* (afternoon snack) or *aperitivo.*

Getting There & Around

Monticchiello is accessed off the SP88, 10km southeast of Pienza. Limited free parking spaces are available next to the historic village gate and there are more spaces in a car park a little way down the hill.

Montepulciano

☎0578 / POP 14,000

Exploring the medieval town of Montepulciano, perched on a reclaimed narrow ridge of volcanic rock, will push your quadriceps to failure point. When this happens, self-medicate with a generous pour of the highly reputed Vino Nobile while also drinking in the spectacular views over the Val di Chiana and Val d'Orcia.

Sights

Il Corso STREET
Montepulciano's main street – called in stages Via di Gracciano, Via di Voltaia, Via dell'Opio and Via Poliziano – climbs up the eastern ridge of the town from Porta al Prato and loops to meet Via di Collazzi on the western ridge. To reach the centre of town (Piazza Grande), take a dog-leg turn into Via del Teatro.

Palazzo Comunale PALACE
(Piazza Grande; terrace & tower adult/reduced €5/2.50, terrace only €2.50; ⊙10am-6pm

Apr-Christmas) Built in the 14th century in Gothic style and remodelled in the 15th century by Michelozzo, the Palazzo Comunale still functions as Montepulciano's town hall. Head up the 67 narrow stairs to the tower to enjoy extraordinary views – you'll see as far as Pienza, Montalcino and even, on a clear day, Siena.

Duomo CATHEDRAL
(Cattedrale di Santa Maria Assunta; www.montepulcianochiusipienza.it; Piazza Grande; 8am-7pm) Montepulciano's 16th-century *duomo* is striking, largely because its unfinished facade gives the building a stern, heavily weathered look. Inside, don't miss Taddeo di Bartolo's ornate *Assumption* triptych (1401) behind the high altar and Sano di Pietro's *Madonna del pilastro* (Madonna of the Pillar; 15th century) on the eastern wall of the nave.

Museo Civico & Pinacoteca Crociani MUSEUM
(0578 71 73 00; www.museocivicomontepulciano.it; Via Ricci 10; adult/reduced €6/4; 10am-6.30pm Wed-Mon Apr-Oct, to 6pm Sat & Sun Nov-Mar) It was a curatorial dream come true: in 2011 a painting in the collection of this modest art gallery was attributed to Caravaggio. The work, *Portrait of a Man*, is thought to portray Cardinal Scipione Borghese, the artist's patron. It's now accompanied by a touch-screen interpretation that allows you to explore details of the painting, its restoration and diagnostic attribution. Other works here include two terracottas by Andrea della Robbia, and Domenico Beccafumi's painting of the town's patron saint, Agnese.

Activities

★**Enoliteca Consortile** WINE
See p24

Cantina de' Ricci WINE
(0578 75 71 66; www.cantinadericci.it; Via Ricci 11; 10.30am-7pm mid-Mar–early Jan, Sat & Sun only early Jan–mid-Mar) FREE The most evocative of Montepulciano's wine cellars, this *cantina* lies at the foot of a steep winding staircase in the Renaissance-era **Palazzo Ricci** (0578 75 60 22; www.palazzoricci.com). Immense vaulted stone encasements surround two-storey-high barrels. Dimly lit and hushed, it's like a cathedral of wine. Entry is free, as will be your first two tastings.

Tours

Strada del Vino Nobile di Montepulciano e dei Sapori della Valdichiana Senese TOURS
(0578 71 74 84; www.stradavinonobile.it; Piazza Grande 7; 9.30am-1.30pm & 2.30-6pm Mon-Fri, 10am-1pm & 2-5pm Sat, 10am-1pm Sun, closed Sat & Sun Jan-Mar) This organisation of local wine and food producers, hospitality businesses and municipalities organises a huge range of tours and courses, including cooking courses (€115 to €170), vineyard tours (€69 to €115) and vineyard walking tours that culminate in wine tasting (€49 to €69). Book in advance online or at its information office.

Sleeping

Camere Bellavista HOTEL €
(0578 75 73 48; www.camerebellavista.it; Via Ricci 25; r €70-120; P) As this budget hotel is four storeys tall and sits on the edge of the old town, the views live up to its name. The styling is heritage rustic with exposed beams, hefty wooden furniture, brass bedsteads and smart new bathrooms. The owner isn't resident, so phone ahead to be met with the key. No breakfast; cash only.

Agriturismo Nobile AGRITURISMO €€
(340 7904752, 347 7252853; www.agriturismonobile.it; Strada per Chianciano, Località San Benedetto; d €100, apt €150-220; P) In the 15th century they were sheds and hen houses; now they're five rustic-chic self-contained apartments. Some have big open fireplaces and many feature grandstand views of Montepulciano, which is only 1km away. There are also five cheaper, simpler rooms in the 15th-century farmhouse; rates for these include breakfast. In high season there's a three-night minimum stay. Very kid-friendly.

Eating & Drinking

Osteria Acquacheta TUSCAN €
(0578 71 70 86; www.acquacheta.eu; Via del Teatro 22; meals €24; 12.30-3pm & 7.30-10.30pm Wed-Mon mid-Apr–Dec) Hugely popular with locals and tourists alike, this bustling *osteria* specialises in *bistecca alla fiorentina* (T-bone steak), which comes to the shared tables in huge, lightly seared and exceptionally flavoursome slabs (don't even *think* of asking for it to be served otherwise). Phone to book ahead.

PHOTOCREO MICHAL BEDNAREK/SHUTTERSTOCK ©

Montepulciano

★**La Dogana** ITALIAN €€
(☎339 5405196; www.ladoganaenoteca.it; Strada Lauretana Nord 75, Valiano; 3-/5-course set lunch €25/40, meals €34; ⏲11am-3.30pm & 6-10pm Wed-Mon, closed Jan) Chef and cookbook writer Sunshine Manitto presides over the kitchen of this chic *enoteca* overlooking the Palazzo Vecchio Winery, 13km northeast of Montepulciano. Windows frame vistas of vines and cypress trees, but the best seats in the house are on the grassed rear terrace. The casual menu showcases seasonal produce (much of it grown in the kitchen garden).

★**La Grotta** TUSCAN €€
(☎0578 75 74 79; www.lagrottamontepulciano.it; Via di San Biagio 15; meals €43; ⏲12.30-2pm & 7.30-10pm Thu-Tue, closed mid-Jan–late Mar) Located just below Montepulciano, overlooking the Renaissance splendour of the Chiesa di San Biago, the town's best restaurant serves traditional dishes with refined flavour and presentation. Service is exemplary, and the courtyard garden is a lovely place to enjoy a six-course tasting menu (€53) or your choice from the à la carte menu. Bookings advisable.

★**Caffè Poliziano** CAFE
(☎0578 75 86 15; www.caffepoliziano.it; Via di Voltaia 27; ⏲7am-9pm Mon-Fri, to 10.30pm Sat, to 9pm Sun; 📶) Established in 1868, Poliziano was lovingly restored to its original form 20 years ago and is the town's most atmospheric cafe. It serves excellent coffee but is most atmospheric for *aperitivo*, when the view of the sun setting over the Val di Chiana from the tables near the rear windows is simply magnificent.

ℹ Information

Strada del Vino Nobile di Montepulciano Information Office (p88) Books accommodation in Montepulciano and arranges a wide range of courses and tours.

Tourist Office (☎0578 75 73 41; www.prolocomontepulciano.it; Piazza Don Minzoni 1; ⏲9.30am-1pm & 3-7pm Apr-Sep, 9.30am-1pm & 3-6pm Mon-Sat Oct-Mar; 📶)

ℹ Getting There & Away

To reach Montepulciano from Florence, take the Valdichiana (Val di Chiana) exit off the A1 (direction Bettolle–Sinalunga) and then follow the signs; from Siena, take the Siena–Bettolle–Perugia Super Strada.

A 24-hour limited traffic zone (ZTL) applies in the historic centre between May and September; in October and April it applies from 8am to 8pm, and from November to March it applies from 8am to 5pm. Check whether your hotel can supply a permit. Otherwise, there are plenty of paid car parks circling the historic centre (€1.50/10 per hour/day).

Assisi & Umbria

With its beautiful historic centre and picturesque surroundings, the birthplace of St Francis welcomes pilgrims of all stripes.

Assisi

POP 28,400

With the plains spreading picturesquely below and Monte Subasio rearing steep and wooded above, the mere sight of Assisi in the rosy glow of dusk is enough to send pilgrims' souls spiralling to heaven. It's at this hour, when the day trippers have left and the town is shrouded in saintly silence, that the true spirit of St Francis of Assisi (p48), born here in 1181, can be felt most keenly. However, you don't have to be religious to be struck by Assisi's beauty and enjoy its pristine *centro storico* (historic centre) and Unesco-listed Basilica di San Francesco, home to one of Italy's most celebrated artistic masterpieces.

Sights

★**Basilica di San Francesco** BASILICA

(www.sanfrancescoassisi.org; Piazza Superiore di San Francesco) FREE Visible for miles around, the Basilica di San Francesco is the crowning glory of Assisi's Unesco-listed historic centre. The 13th-century complex is comprised of two churches: the Gothic **Basilica Superiore** (Upper Church; 8.30am-6.50pm summer, to 6pm winter), with its celebrated cycle of Giotto frescoes, and beneath, the older **Basilica Inferiore** (Lower Church; 6am-6.50pm summer, to 6.10pm winter) where you'll find works by Cimabue, Pietro Lorenzetti and Simone Martini. Also here, in the **Cripta di San Francesco**, is St Francis' much venerated tomb.

Foro Romano ROMAN SITE

(Roman Forum; 848 004000; www.coopculture.it; Via Portica 2; adult/reduced €5/3, incl Rocca Maggiore €9/6; 10am-7pm summer, to 5pm winter) In among the churches and medieval streets you can still find a few traces of Assisi's Roman past. Extending beneath Piazza del Commune are the remains of the town's ancient forum, discovered during archaeological digs in the 19th century. Above ground, the piazza is dominated by the columned facade of the 1st-century-BC **Tempio di Minerva** (Temple of Minerva; 7am-7.30pm Mon-Sat, from 8am Sun) FREE, that now hides a rather uninspiring 16th-century church.

Cattedrale di San Rufino CHURCH

(Piazza San Rufino; 7.30am-7pm) This 13th-century Romanesque church, remodelled by Galeazzo Alessi in the 16th century, contains the font where St Francis and St Clare were baptised. The square facade, punctuated by three doors and three rose windows, is adorned with grotesque figures and fantastic animals.

Rocca Maggiore FORT
(☎848 004000; www.coopculture.it; Via della Rocca; adult/reduced €6/4, incl Foro Romano €9/6; ⏲10am-8pm, shorter hours winter) Looming over Assisi is the 14th-century Rocca Maggiore, an oft-expanded, pillaged and rebuilt fortress that commands inspiring 360-degree views of Perugia to the north and the surrounding valleys below. Walk up winding staircases and claustrophobic passageways to reach the archer slots that served the Assisians as they fought off various medieval invaders.

Activities

To experience Assisi's spirituality, do as St Francis did and take to the surrounding wooded hills. Popular walks include the 4km-trek to the **Eremo delle Carceri** (☎075 81 23 01; www.eremodellecarceri.it; Via Eremo delle Carceri; ⏲6.30am-7pm Mon-Sat, from 7.30pm Sun summer, to 6pm winter) FREE and the downhill stroll to the **Chiesa di San Damiano** (☎075 81 22 73; www.santuariosandamiano.org; Via San Damiano 7; ⏲10am-noon & 2-6pm summer, to 4.30pm winter). The tourist office (p94) can provide information on routes, including paths in the nearby **Monte Subasio** and St Francis' Way, a long, multi-leg trail that traverses Umbria.

Bicycle rentals are available at **Angelucci Cicli** (☎075 804 25 50, 393 1304680; www.angeluccicicli.it; Via Risorgimento 54a; bike hire per hour/day €5/20, e-bike €13/39; ⏲8.30am-12.30pm & 3.30-7.30pm Mon-Sat) in Assisi's suburb of Santa Maria degli Angeli.

Sleeping

There's plenty of accommodation in Assisi, but you'll still need to book well in advance for peak periods such as Easter, August, September and the **Festa di San Francesco** (3 and 4 October). The tourist office (p94) can provide a list of private rooms, religious institutions, flats and *agriturismi* (farm-stay accommodation) in and around Assisi.

Hotel Alexander HOTEL €
(☎075 81 61 90; www.hotelalexanderassisi.it; Piazza Chiesa Nuova 6; s €55-75, d €75-110, ste €120-140; ❄📶) On a small cobbled piazza by the Chiesa Nuova, this attractive hideaway offers nine spacious rooms and a communal terrace with wonderful rooftop views. The modern decor – pale wooden floors and earthy brown tones – contrasts well with the wood-beamed ceilings and carefully preserved antiquity all around.

Alla Madonna del Piatto AGRITURISMO €
(☎328 7025297; www.incampagna.com; Via Petrata 37, Pieve San Nicolò; d €90, apt for 2/4/6 people per week €650/700/750; ⏲Mar-Nov; P) 🍃 Waking up to views of lush green meadows and olive groves will put a spring in your step at this ecofriendly *agriturismo*, less than 15 minutes' drive from

CRIS FOTO/SHUTTERSTOCK ©

Basilica di San Francesco

Assisi

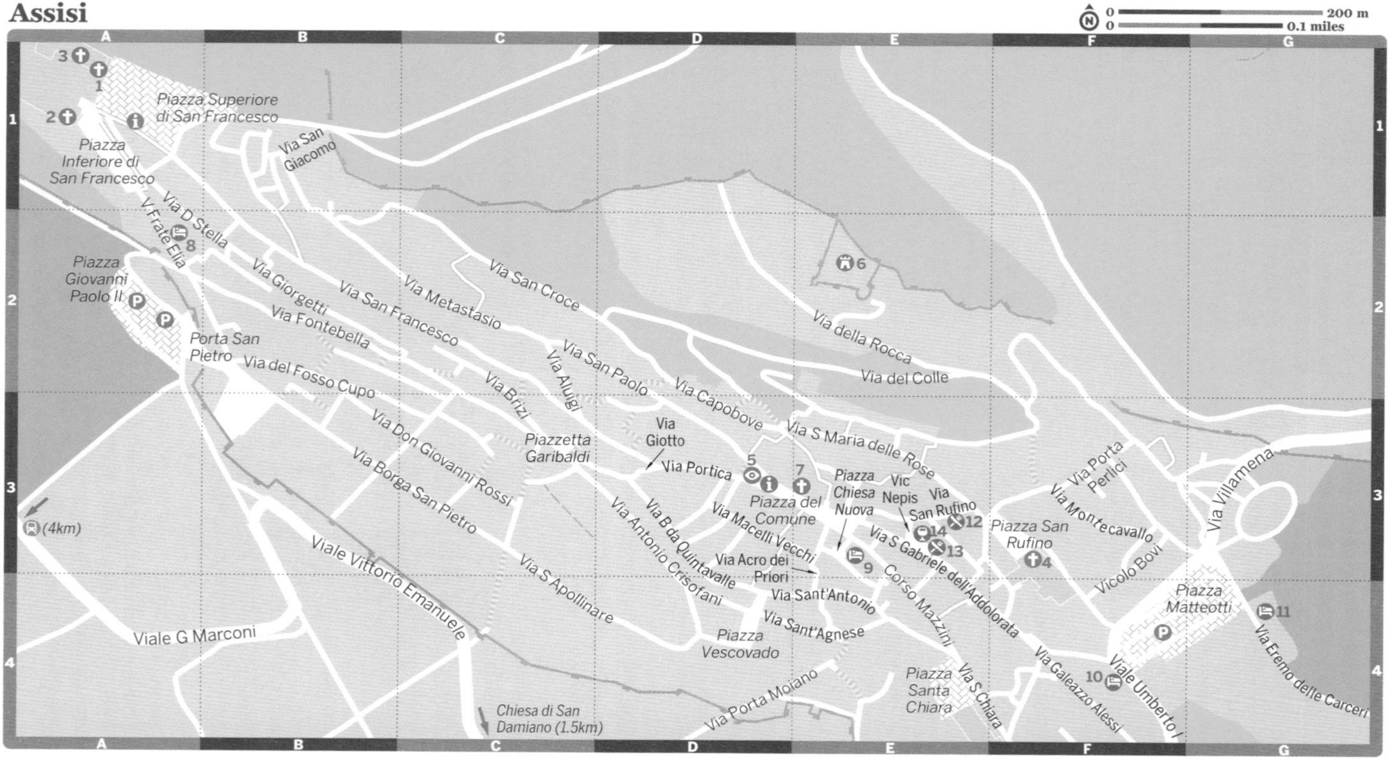

0 — 200 m
0 — 0.1 miles

Piazza Superiore di San Francesco
Piazza Inferiore di San Francesco
Via San Giacomo
Via D Stella
V Frate Elia
Piazza Giovanni Paolo II
Porta San Pietro
Via Giorgetti
Via Fontebella
Via San Francesco
Via Metastasio
Via San Croce
Via del Fosso Cupo
Via Brizi
Via Aluigi
Via San Paolo
Via Capobove
Via della Rocca
Via del Colle
Via S Maria delle Rose
Via Don Giovanni Rossi
Via Borga San Pietro
Piazzetta Garibaldi
Via Giotto
Via Portica
Piazza del Comune
Piazza Chiesa Nuova
Vic Nepis
Via San Rufino
Piazza San Rufino
Via Porta Perlici
Via Montecavallo
Via Villamena
Vicolo Bovi
Piazza Matteotti
Via Eremo delle Carceri
Viale Umberto I
Via Galeazzo Alessi
Via S Chiara
Piazza Santa Chiara
Corso Mazzini
Via S Gabriele dell'Addolorata
Via Macelli Vecchi
Via Acro dei Priori
Via Sant'Antonio
Via Sant'Agnese
Piazza Vescovado
Via B da Quintavalle
Via Antonio Crisofani
Via S Apollinare
Via Porta Moiano
Viale Vittorio Emanuele
Viale G Marconi
(4km)
Chiesa di San Damiano (1.5km)

Assisi

Sights

1 Basilica di San Francesco A1
2 Basilica Inferiore A1
3 Basilica Superiore A1
4 Cattedrale di San Rufino F3
5 Foro Romano D3
6 Rocca Maggiore E2
7 Tempio di Minerva E3

Sleeping

8 Gallery Hotel Sorella Luna A2
9 Hotel Alexander E3
10 Hotel Ideale F4
11 Nun Assisi G4

Eating

12 Hostaria Terra Chiama E3
Osteria Eat Out ..... (see 11)
13 Osteria La Piazzetta dell'Erba E3

Drinking & Nightlife

14 Bibenda Assisi E3

Assisi. Its six rooms and spacious self-catering apartment have all been tastefully designed and feature wrought-iron beds, antique furnishings and intricate handmade fabrics. Note there's a minimum two-night stay.

★Gallery Hotel Sorella Luna HOTEL €€
(075 81 61 94; www.hotelsorellaluna.it; Via Frate Elia 3; r €53-150;) This artistic hideaway, ideally located about 200m from the Basilica di San Francesco and five minutes' walk from the Parcheggio Piazza Giovanni Paolo II, is a real find. Its 15 rooms are bright and tastefully low-key with clean white walls, unobtrusive modern furniture and smooth brick-tiled floors. Breakfast is a further plus and well worth getting up for.

Hotel Ideale HOTEL €€
(075 81 35 70; www.hotelideale.it; Piazza Matteotti 1; s €40-60, d €75-145; P) Ideal indeed, this welcoming family-run hotel is conveniently located near the bus stops on Piazza Matteotti. Many of its bright, simply decorated rooms open onto balconies with uplifting views over the rooftops to the valley beyond. Breakfast is done properly, with fresh pastries, fruit, cold cuts and frothy cappuccino, and is served in the garden when the weather's fine.

★Nun Assisi BOUTIQUE HOTEL €€€
(075 815 51 50; www.nunassisi.com; Via Eremo delle Carceri 1a; s €285-335, d €350-400, ste €325-450; P) An air of Zen-like calm hangs over this super-stylish boutique hotel. Housed in a converted stone convent, it exudes understated class with a decor that elegantly pairs original trappings with a clean, modern aesthetic. Stone arches and wood beams feature alongside discreet mod cons and minimalist furniture in the cool, pared-down rooms.

Eating & Drinking

Terra Umbra Antica SANDWICHES €
(075 804 36 96; Via Patrono d'Italia 10; panini €2-3; 8am-1pm & 4-7.30pm Mon-Sat, to 7pm Sun) A fat, well-stuffed *panino,* perhaps with tangy *pecorino* cheese or sweet *prosciutto crudo* (Parma ham), makes for a handy, on-the-hoof lunch. This small food shop near the basilica in Santa Maria degli Angeli prepares them on the spot, as well as serving platters of cheese and cured meats and selling Umbrian wines, olive oils, conserves and pastas.

★Osteria La Piazzetta dell'Erba OSTERIA €€
(075 81 53 52; www.osterialapiazzetta.it; Via San Gabriele dell'Addolorata 15a; meals €30-35; 12.30-2.30pm & 7.30-10pm Tue-Sun;) Tables at this local favourite are always coveted: in winter in the cosy stone-vaulted interior, in summer outside on a small, flower-strewn square. The big draw is the kitchen's inventive cuisine and a seasonally driven menu that's flecked with Asian and European influences (hummus, sauerkraut and wasabi regularly pop up in dishes).

★Osteria Eat Out GASTRONOMY €€
(075 81 31 63; www.eatoutosteriagourmet.it; Via Eremo delle Carceri 1a; meals €50, tasting menu €110; 7.30-10.30pm daily, plus 12.30-2.30pm Sat & Sun;) With its dreamy alfresco terrace and casually chic interiors, you might expect the glass-fronted restaurant of the five-star Nun Assisi hotel to be all style over substance. Not so. Polished service and an exciting wine list are well matched by chef Emanuele Mazzella's refined and creative take on seasonal Italian cuisine.

Hostaria Terra Chiama OSTERIA €€
(075 819 90 51; www.hostariaterrachiama.it; Via San Rufino 16; meals €25-35; 11am-11pm;)

Annarita is your hospitable host at this casual, brick-arched *osteria,* where enquiries for a glass of local red are met with a barrage of tasting options. Its menu, designed to showcase regional ingredients, tempts with simple but honed preparations like pasta with Norcia black truffles and pork shank with roast potatoes.

Bibenda Assisi WINE BAR
(☎075 815 51 76; www.bibendaassisi.it; Vicolo Nepis 9; wines by the glass from €3.50; ⏱11.30am-11pm Wed-Mon; 📶) Aficionados and wine enthusiasts love this inviting, rustic-chic bar. Owner Nila, a highly knowledgeable Ukrainian transplant, will talk you through the wine list she has assembled from small, boutique producers and tiny appellations – all served in proper Riedel glassware and paired with tasting platters of local *salumi e formaggi* (cured meats and cheese). At busy times, call ahead to reserve a table.

Information

Tourist Office (☎075 813 86 80; www.visit-assisi.it; Piazza del Comune 10; ⏱9am-7pm) Stop by here for maps, leaflets and accommodation lists.

Getting There & Around

CAR & MOTORCYCLE

To reach Assisi from Perugia take the SS75, exit at Ospedalicchio and follow the signs.

Daytime parking is all but banned in Assisi's historic centre, but there are convenient car parks just outside the old town at **Piazza Giovanni Paolo II** (www.sabait.it; per hour €1.25; ⏱24hr) – the closest to the basilica – and **Piazza Matteotti** (www.sabait.it; per hour €1.30; ⏱24hr).

TAXI

For a taxi, call **Radio Taxi Assisi** (☎075 81 31 00; www.radiotaxiassisi.it).

Perugia

POP 165,700

With a pristine medieval centre and an international student population, Perugia is Umbria's largest and most cosmopolitan city. Its *centro storico* (historic centre), seemingly little changed in more than 400 years, rises in a helter-skelter of cobbled alleys, arched stairways and piazzas framed by solemn churches and magnificent Gothic *palazzi* (mansions). Reminders of its lively and often bloody past are everywhere, from ancient arches and medieval basilicas to Renaissance frescoes by the likes of Perugino and Raphael.

But while history reverberates all around, Perugia knows how to party. University students pep up the nightlife and fill cafe terraces, while music-lovers swarm to the city in July for **Umbria Jazz**, one of Europe's top jazz festivals.

Sights

Cattedrale di San Lorenzo CATHEDRAL
(☎075 572 38 32; Piazza IV Novembre; ⏱7.30am-12.30pm & 3.30-6.45pm Mon-Sat, 8am-12.45pm & 4-7pm Sun) Lording it over Piazza IV Novembre is a stark medieval cathedral. A church has stood here since the 900s, but the version you see today was begun in 1345 from designs created by Fra Bevignate. Building continued until 1587, although the main facade was never completed. Inside you'll find dramatic late-Gothic architecture, an altarpiece by Signorelli and sculptures by Duccio. The steps in front of the facade are where seemingly all of Perugia congregates; they overlook the pink-and-white **Fontana Maggiore**.

★**Palazzo dei Priori** HISTORIC BUILDING
(Corso Vannucci 19) Flanking Corso Vannucci, this Gothic palace, constructed between the 13th and 14th centuries, is architecturally striking with its tripartite windows, ornamental portal and fortress-like crenellations. It was formerly the headquarters of the local magistracy, but now houses the city's main art gallery, the Galleria Nazionale dell'Umbria, and a series of historic rooms and suites: the Nobile Collegio del Cambio; the **Nobile Collegio della Mercanzia** (Merchant's Hall; ☎075 573 03 66; www.collegiomercanzia.it; €1.50, incl Nobile Collegio del Cambio €5.50; ⏱9am-1pm & 2.30-5.30pm Tue-Sat & 9am-1pm Sun summer, shorter hours winter); and the **Sala dei Notari** (Notaries' Hall; ⏱9am-1pm & 3-7pm Tue-Sun) FREE.

★**Galleria Nazionale dell'Umbria** GALLERY
(☎075 572 10 09; www.gallerianazionaleumbria.it; Palazzo dei Priori, Corso Vannucci 19; adult/reduced €8/4; ⏱8.30am-7.30pm Tue-Sun year-round, plus from noon Mon mid-Mar–Oct) Umbria's foremost art gallery is housed in Palazzo dei Priori on Perugia's main strip. Its collection, chronologically displayed over 40 rooms, is one of central Italy's finest, numbering more than 3000 works, that range from Byzantine-inspired

DREVS/SHUTTERSTOCK ©

Street performers, Perugia

13th-century paintings to Gothic works by Gentile da Fabriano and Renaissance masterpieces by home-town heroes Pinturicchio and Perugino. Important works include Gentile da Fabriano's *Madonna con il bambino e angeli* (early 15th century), the *Pala di Santa Maria dei Fossi* altarpiece (1496–98) by Pinturicchio, and Benedetto Bonfigli's fresco cycle for the *Cappella dei priori* (c 1454–80).

★Nobile Collegio del Cambio HISTORIC BUILDING
(Exchange Hall; ☎075 572 85 99; www.collegiodelcambio.it; Palazzo dei Priori, Corso Vannucci 25; €4.50, incl Nobile Collegio della Mercanzia €5.50; ⏱9am-12.30pm & 2.30-5.30pm Mon-Sat, 9am-1pm Sun) Seat of Perugia's Moneychanger's Guild between 1452 and 1457, the extravagantly adorned Nobile Collegio del Cambio has three rooms: the **Sala dei Legisti** (Jurists' Hall), with 17th-century wooden stalls carved by Giampiero Zuccari; the **Sala dell'Udienza** (Audience Chamber), with inlaid wooden furniture and outstanding Renaissance frescoes by Perugino; and the **Cappella di San Giovanni Battista** (Chapel of San Giovanni Battista), painted by a student of Perugino's, Giannicola di Paolo.

Tours

Studio Moretti Caselli ART
(☎340 7765594; www.studiomoretticaselli.it; Via Fatebenefratelli 2; tour contribution per person €5; ⏱10am-12.30pm Tue & Wed or by appt) Explore the colourful world of stained glass on a tour of this family-run studio. It was originally founded in 1860 by master glasspainter Francesco Moretti, whose work peppers historic churches and buildings in Perugia, throughout Italy and across the world.

Sleeping

B&B San Fiorenzo B&B €
(☎393 3869987; www.sanfiorenzo.com; Via Alessi 45; d €70-90, q €100-120, apt per week €450-560; 📶) Buried in Perugia's medieval centre is this charming B&B, where Luigi and Monica make you welcome in one of three suites, each with its independent entrance. Mod cons and marble bathrooms have been skilfully incorporated into spacious quarters with brick vaulting, lime-washed walls and antique furnishings; the Maior suite even has a shower built into an 11th-century well.

Hotel Rosalba HOTEL €
(☎075 572 82 85; www.hotelrosalbaperugia.com; Piazza del Circo 7; s €47-65, d €55-75, q €90-100; ❄📶) An inviting budget option, the two-star Rosalba occupies a hard-to-miss pink town house just off the escalator up from Piazza Partigiana. Facilities are modest but its clean, simply attired rooms offer top value for money. The best come with balconies and views, though one, downstairs, is a tad dark. Breakfast is €4.50 extra.

Hotel Fortuna HISTORIC HOTEL €€
(☎075 573 50 40; www.hotelfortunaperugia.com; Via Luigi Bonazzi 19; s €70-90, d €80-150,

Perugia

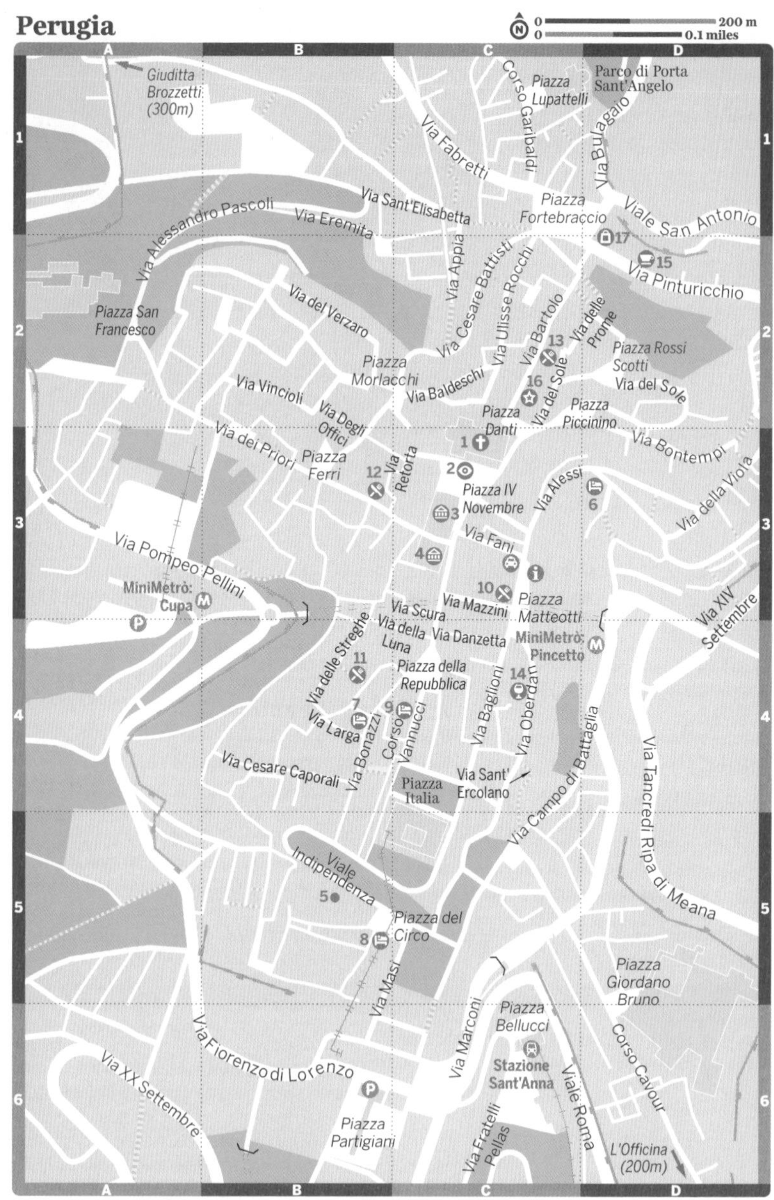

tr €135-180, q €170-220; ❄@📶) Behind a weathered stone facade draped in ivy, this historic three-star hotel hides 14th-century walls and secrets like its former past as a love motel. Past the welcoming front desk, you'll find original frescoes on the 3rd floor, Murano chandeliers in the breakfast room and classic decor that instils a sense of place in its 52 guest rooms.

★ **Castello di Monterone** HOTEL €€€
(☎075 572 42 14; www.castellomonterone.com; Strada Montevile 3; r €110-250; P❄📶🏊) This fairy-tale castle comes with all the turreted,

Perugia

Sights

1 Cattedrale di San Lorenzo C3
2 Fontana Maggiore C3
3 Galleria Nazionale dell'Umbria C3
4 Nobile Collegio del Cambio C3
Nobile Collegio della Mercanzia .... (see 3)
Palazzo dei Priori .... (see 3)
Sala dei Notari .... (see 3)

Activities, Courses & Tours

5 Studio Moretti Caselli B5

Sleeping

6 B&B San Fiorenzo D3
7 Hotel Fortuna B4
8 Hotel Rosalba B5
9 Locanda della Posta C4

Eating

10 Antica Salumeria Granieri Amato C3
11 La Taverna B4
12 Osteria a Priori B3
13 Società Anonima C2

Drinking & Nightlife

14 Kundera C4
15 Pinturicchio Cafe & Kitchen D2

Entertainment

16 Marla C2

Shopping

17 Augusta Perusia Cioccolato e Gelateria D2

ivy-clad, vaulted trappings you would imagine. Its 18 individually designed rooms have been finished to great effect, with low timber-beamed ceilings, exposed stone, custom wood furniture, handmade wrought-iron beds, antiques and the odd Etruscan and medieval artefact. Superior rooms come with views over the rolling countryside to Perugia's centre, 3km away.

★Locanda della Posta BOUTIQUE HOTEL €€€
(075 572 89 25; www.locandadellapostahotel.it; Corso Vannucci 97; d €130-280, ste €200-500; ❄@📶) Perugia's oldest hotel dates from 1786, but a complete 2017 makeover turned it into one of the city's sleekest digs. Stunning 18th-century frescoes juxtapose with glistening marble flooring, contemporary art and a minimalist grey-and-white colour scheme. None of the 17 rooms are the same, but modish elements like hardwood flooring and textured shower walls feature in several.

Eating

★Antica Salumeria Granieri Amato SANDWICHES €
(Piazza Matteotti; sandwiches €3-4.50, with glass of wine €5; ⏲11am-8pm Mon-Sat, hours vary Sun) Sitting inconspicuously in a no-fanfare grey kiosk on Piazza Matteotti is this Perugian street-food institution. Its speciality is succulent *porchetta* (herbed roast pork) piled high and served – crispy skin and all – in a crusty bread roll for €4.50. Get in line and *buon appetito*!

Società Anonima GASTROPUB €
(075 572 18 99; www.societaanonimaperugia.it; Via Bartolo 25; panini €6-7, 4-/6-course menus €30/40; ⏲7.30pm-12.30am Thu-Tue; 📶) Local food-and-wine enthusiasts Paolo Baldelli and Antonio Boco offer something different at this trendy gastro-bar, urbanely housed in an old ice factory. Sit at the long, black bar or a table by the exposed stone wall and dig into gourmet snacks and creative mains.

★L'Officina UMBRIAN €€
(075 572 16 99; www.l-officina.net; Borgo XX Giugno 56; meals €30-35, 6-course tasting menus €25-40; ⏲12.30-3.30pm & 6.30-midnight Mon-Sat; 📶) Gourmet food at everyday prices make L'Officina one of Perugia's hottest dining tickets. Passionate owner Yannis shares his 30 years of Italian food and wine experience at this, his meandering restaurant set inside a former factory. The vibe is casual and the food modern and exciting with seasonally driven menus (including a vegetarian tasting menu) and inventive, artfully presented dishes.

★La Taverna RISTORANTE €€
(075 572 41 28; www.ristorantelataverna.com; Via delle Streghe 8; meals €35-40; ⏲12.30-2.30pm & 7.30-10.30pm; 📶) La Taverna consistently wins the praise of local foodies. Brick vaults and candlelit tables create an intimate backdrop for Chef Claudio Brugolossi's seasonal dishes, from homemade ravioli with black truffles to a bevy of diverse *secondi* (expertly grilled steaks, lamb stew with flat bread, chicken curry), all paired with superb wines.

KIRSHU/SHUTTERSTOCK ©

Orvieto

★**Osteria a Priori** UMBRIAN €€

(☎075 572 70 98; www.osteriaapriori.it; Via dei Priori 39; meals €30-35; ⊙12.30-2.30pm & 7.30-10pm Mon-Sat; ☎) Located above an *enoteca* (wine bar/shop), this fashionable *osteria* (tavern) specialises in local wines and fresh regional cuisine prepared with seasonal ingredients. Umbrian cheeses and cured meats feature alongside black truffles, Chianina beef and autumnal mushrooms. Reservations recommended.

Drinking & Nightlife

★**Pinturicchio Cafe & Kitchen** CAFE

(☎340 4610715; www.pinturicchiocafe.com; Via Pinturicchio 26; ⊙8am-midnight Mon, to 1.30am Tue-Fri, 3pm-1.30am Sat, 11am-3pm Sun) This cool hang-out draws a steady stream of students and trendy urbanites throughout the day, for coffee and bagels at breakfast, light lunches, craft beers on tap and wines by the glass. Mismatched furniture and lived-in sofas create a relaxed living-room vibe, while regular events ensure there's always something going on.

★**Kundera** BAR

(☎075 372 54 35; www.facebook.com/KunderaCaffeBistrot; Via Oberdan 23; ⊙6.30pm-11pm Tue-Thu & Sun, to midnight Fri, to 1am Sat; ☎) Follow the lead of students and clued-up locals by searching out this artsy little backstreet bar for an early evening *aperitivo*. Until 9.30pm you can pair a drink (including a fine €4.50 spritz) with your choice of tasty appetiser platters (up to €5) – you can even ask for vegetarian and gluten-free options. Snag a table on the terrace when it's warm.

Entertainment

Some of the venues and clubs in the outskirts of town run a shuttle bus to/from the Università per Stranieri, starting around 11pm. Students hand out flyers on Corso Vannucci, so check with them or ask at the steps. Most places get going around midnight, so it's worth remembering that the *scale mobili* (escalators) stop running at 2am.

Marla LIVE MUSIC

(☎347 1878420; www.facebook.com/marla.perugia; Via Bartolo 9; ⊙8pm-1.30am Tue-Sat; ☎) A favourite among a 30s and 40s alternative crowd, this bohemian haunt hosts acts from across the musical spectrum (jazz, rock, soul, reggae, electronic) as well as art installations and mismatched vintage furniture. DJs spin house, techno and/or disco on Saturdays. The music generally gets going around 10.30pm to 11pm.

Shopping

Giuditta Brozzetti ARTS & CRAFTS

(☎075 4 02 36; www.brozzetti.com; Via Tiberio Berardi 5; ⊙by appt 8.30am-12.30pm & 3-6pm Mon-Fri) Inside a 13th-century Franciscan church, fourth-generation weaver Marta Cucchia is one of the few artisans still working with 19th-century jacquard looms. Her extraordinary and fascinating workshop resurrects previously lost medieval and Renaissance textile styles and patterns – some seen in Leonardo da Vinci's *The Last Supper* – weaving them into everything from bookmarks and cushions to table runners and custom-made tablecloths.

Marta also leads guided group tours of the workshop, available in English on request.

Augusta Perusia Cioccolato e Gelateria CHOCOLATE
(☎075 573 45 77; www.cioccolatoaugustaperusia.it; Via Pinturicchio 2; per 100g €6; ⏰10.30am-8pm; 👪) Founded in 2000 by Giacomo Mangano, an expert chocolatier who learned his craft at Casa del Cioccolato Perugina, Augusta Perusia is a renowned chocolate maker. This, the company's original shop, is a magical showroom for all sorts of chocolatey delights, from slabs of rich dark choc spiked with zesty candied orange to melt-in-your-mouth pralines and creamy spreads.

DON'T MISS

PERUGIA'S HOUSE OF CHOCOLATE

To visit the Wonka-esque world of Perugian chocolate, sign up for a 1¼-hour guided tour (in Italian or English; times vary) of the **Casa del Cioccolato Perugina** (☎800 800 907; www.perugina.it; Van San Sisto 207, Località San Sisto; adult/reduced €9/7; ⏰9am-1pm & 2-5.30pm Mon-Fri, 10am-4pm Sat; 👪) FREE. After visiting the museum, you'll wend your way through an enclosed sky bridge, watching as the white-outfitted Oompa Loompas, er, factory workers, go about their chocolate-creating business.

The Casa is located at Nestlé's large, nondescript factory in the outskirts of town – drive through the factory entrance, or take the bus to San Sisto (€1.50, 25 minutes).

Information

Ospedale S. Maria della Misericordia (☎075 57 81; www.ospedale.perugia.it; Piazza Menghini 1, Località Sant'Andrea delle Fratte; ⏰24hr) Perugia's main hospital, 7km southwest of the city centre.

Tourist Office (☎075 573 64 58; http://turismo.comune.perugia.it; Piazza Matteotti 18; ⏰9am-6pm) Housed in the 14th-century Loggia dei Lanari, Perugia's main tourist office has stacks of info on the city, including maps (€0.50) and guides (€2.50), and can provide up-to-date bus and train timetables.

Getting There & Around

AIR

Umbria International Airport San Francesco d'Assisi (☎075 59 21 41; www.airport.umbria.it; Via dell'Aeroporto, Sant'Egidio), 12km east of the city, is served by Ryanair flights to/from London, Brussels, Catania and Malta; and Albawings and Blu-Express flights to/from Tirana.

CAR & MOTORCYCLE

To reach Perugia from Rome, leave the A1 at the Orte exit and follow signs for Terni. Once there, take the SS3bis/E45 for Perugia. From the north, exit the A1 at Valdichiana and take dual-carriageway RA6 *(raccordo autostradale)*. To the east of Perugia, the SS75 connects the city with Assisi.

Rental companies have offices at the airport and **train station** (Perugia Fontivegge; ☎075 963 78 91; Piazza Vittorio Veneto).

Perugia is notoriously difficult to navigate and much of the historic centre is off-limits to unauthorised traffic. Your best bet is to leave your car in one of the big, signposted car parks (€1.10 to €1.90 per hour; open 24 hours) – Piazza Partigiani and the Mercato Coperto are the most convenient.

TAXI

Call **Radio Taxi Perugia** (☎075 500 48 88; www.perugiataxi.it; ⏰24hrs) to arrange a pick-up. A ride from the city centre to the main train station will cost about €10 to €15. Tack on €1 for each suitcase.

Orvieto

POP 20,300

Set atop a gigantic plug of rock above fields streaked with vines, olive groves and cypress trees, Orvieto is one of Umbria's star attractions. Its austere medieval centre is a classic of its kind, with weaving lanes, brown stone houses and cobbled piazzas, and its location between Rome and Florence ensures a constant stream of visitors. But what sets the town apart from its medieval neighbours is its breathtaking cathedral. This extraordinary vision, one of Italy's greatest Gothic churches, is stunning inside and out, with a sensational facade and frescoes that are

Orvieto

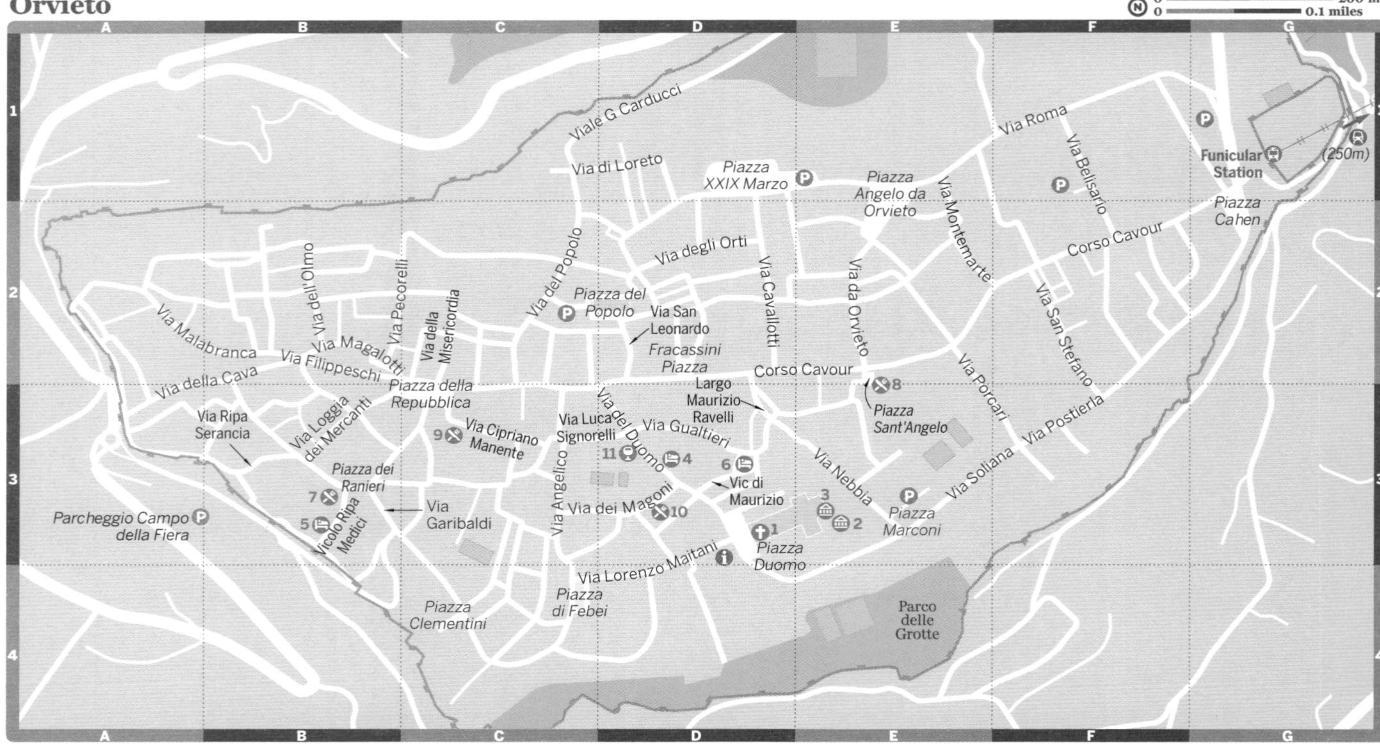
0 200 m
0 0.1 miles
Via Roma
Funicular Station
(250m)
Piazza Cahen
Via Belisario
Corso Cavour
Via San Stefano
Via Montemarte
Via Porcari
Via Postierla
Via Soliana
Piazza Angelo da Orvieto
Via da Orvieto
Piazza Sant'Angelo
Piazza Marconi
Parco delle Grotte
Via Nebbia
Piazza Duomo
Piazza XXIX Marzo
Via Cavallotti
Via degli Orti
Largo Maurizio Ravelli
Vic di Maurizio
Via Gualtieri
Via di Loreto
Viale G Carducci
Via del Popolo
Piazza del Popolo
Via San Leonardo
Fracassini Piazza
Via del Duomo
Via dei Magoni
Via Lorenzo Maitani
Via Luca Signorelli
Via Angelico
Piazza di Febei
Via Cipriano Manente
Piazza della Repubblica
Via della Misericordia
Via Pecorelli
Via Garibaldi
Piazza Clementini
Piazza dei Ranieri
Via Loggia dei Mercanti
Vicolo Ripa Medici
Via dell'Olmo
Via Magalotti
Via Filippeschi
Via Malabranca
Via della Cava
Via Ripa Serancia
Parcheggio Campo della Fiera
A
B
C
D
E
F
G
1
2
3
4
1
2
3
4
5
6
7
8
9
10
11

Orvieto

said by some to rival Michelangelo's in the Sistine Chapel.

Sights

★Duomo CATHEDRAL
(☎0763 34 24 77; www.opsm.it; Piazza Duomo 26; €4, incl Museo dell'Opera del Duomo di Orvieto €5; ⏰9.30am-7pm Mon-Sat, 1-5.30pm Sun summer, shorter hours winter) Nothing can prepare you for the visual feast that is Orvieto's soul-stirring Gothic cathedral. Dating from 1290, it sports a black-and-white banded exterior fronted by what is perhaps the most astonishing facade to grace any Italian church: a mesmerising display of rainbow frescoes, jewel-like mosaics, bas-reliefs and delicate braids of flowers and vines. Head inside and the show continues, most spectacularly in the form of Luca Signorelli's mesmerising *Giudizio universale* (Last Judgement) fresco in the **Cappella di San Brizio**.

The building took 30 years to plan and three centuries to complete. It was started by Fra Bevignate and later additions were made by Sienese master Lorenzo Maitani, Andrea Pisano (of Florence Cathedral fame) and his son Nino, Andrea Orcagna and Michele Sanmicheli.

Museo dell'Opera del Duomo di Orvieto MUSEUM
(☎0763 34 24 77; www.opsm.it; Piazza Duomo 26; €4, incl Duomo €5; ⏰9.30am-7pm daily summer, to 5pm Tue-Sun winter) Housed in a complex of papal palaces, the Palazzi Papali, this museum showcases a fine collection of religious relics from the *duomo* and paintings by artists such as Arnolfo di Cambio and the three Pisanos (Andrea, Nino and Giovanni). A separate exhibition in Palazzo Soliano is dedicated to sculptor and medallist Emilio Greco (1913–95).

The ticket also covers admission to the former **Chiesa di Sant'Agostino** (Piazza San Giovenale) where the museum's sculptural collection is on show.

Museo Archeologico Nazionale MUSEUM
(☎0763 34 10 39; Palazzo Papale, Piazza Duomo; adult/reduced €4/2; ⏰8.30am-7.30pm) Housed in the medieval Palazzo Papale behind the *duomo*, Orvieto's archaeological museum holds plenty of interesting artefacts, some over 2500 years old. Etruscan ceramics, necropolis relics, bronzes and frescoed chamber tombs feature among the items on display.

Sleeping

★B&B Ripa Medici B&B €
(☎328 7469620, 0763 34 13 43; www.ripamedici.com; Vicolo Ripa Medici 14; s €50, d €75-90; P❄📶) Hugging the walls on the edge of Orvieto's old town, this gracious B&B takes the concept of a 'room with a view' to another level, gazing out across undulating countryside. But the dreamy views are just one of its attractions. The immaculate guest room and two apartments ooze charm and are lovingly furnished with antique pieces, timber beams and English farmhouse decor.

B&B La Magnolia B&B €
(☎349 4620733, 0763 34 28 08; www.bblamagnolia.it; Via del Duomo 29; s €45-60, d €60-85, apt €55-140; ❄📶) A short hop from the Duomo, this lovely B&B makes a handy base for the historic centre. It's a relaxed set-up with four light-filled rooms and three apartments, all decorated in simple, cosy style and some boasting original 18th-century frescoes. The English-speaking owner Serena extends a friendly welcome and is a mine of local information.

★Misia Resort BOUTIQUE HOTEL €€
(☎0763 34 23 36; www.misiaresort.it; Località Rocca Ripesena 51; s/d/ste €80/130/160; P❄📶) You won't regret going the extra mile to this boutique hotel in Rocca Ripesena, a panoramic hilltop hamlet 6km west of Orvieto. Its light, spacious rooms and suites, in the main hotel building and spread across the stone village, feature soft, earthy tones and

stylish vintage touches – a chesterfield sofa here, a distressed wood beam there.

Hotel Duomo HOTEL €€
(☎0763 34 18 87; www.orvietohotelduomo.com; Vicolo di Maurizio 7; s €70-90, d €100-130, ste €120-150; P ❄ @ 🛜) Bunk down in the shadow of the *duomo* at this friendly three-star where the church bells will most likely be your wake-up call. Orvieto-born artist Livio Orazio Valentini has left bold, abstract paintings in some of the 18 guest rooms, which are tastefully decorated in polished woods and subdued cream colours.

Eating

Umbrichelli, a thick, spaghetti-like pasta, served *all'arrabbiata* (with spicy tomato sauce), stews of wild boar and – like most of Umbria – truffled *everything* are just a few of the delicacies that pair nicely with the town's renowned DOC wines.

Trattoria La Palomba UMBRIAN €
(☎0763 34 33 95; Via Cipriano Manente 16; meals €30-35; ⏲12.30-2.15pm & 7.30-10pm Thu-Tue; 🛜) If you want to know what a genuine Italian trattoria experience is all about, head to this family-run local favourite. Wood panelling and old-school house wine labels abound, and the food – heavy on homemade pastas, hearty game sauces and aromatic local truffles – hits the spot perfectly. Bookings highly recommended.

Trattoria La Pergola TRATTORIA €€
(☎0763 34 30 65; www.lapergolaorvieto.com; Via dei Magoni 9B; meals €25-30; ⏲12.15-3pm & 7.15-10pm Thu-Tue) This charming backstreet trattoria disproves any theories that you can't eat well near major tourist sites. A family-run outfit, it cooks up hearty regional food near the *duomo*, serving the likes of gnocchi with bacon, spinach and truffle sauce, and casseroled wild boar, in a cosy front room or a walled courtyard at the back.

Al Pozzo Etrusco UMBRIAN €€
(☎0763 34 10 50; www.alpozzoetruscodagiovanni.it; Piazza dei Ranieri 1a; meals €30-35; ⏲12.30-2.30pm & 7.30-9.30pm Wed-Mon; 🛜) Named after an ancient Etruscan well that graces its basement, this is a firm local favourite. Your host, Giovanni, will guide you through his seasonal menu of updated Umbrian delights, best enjoyed alfresco on the charming candlelit terrace. Pastas are seasoned with herbed meats and flavoursome vegetables, paving the way for original mains such as beef cheeks stewed in red beer.

★I Sette Consoli ITALIAN €€€
(☎0763 34 39 11; www.isetteconsoli.it; Piazza Sant'Angelo 1a; meals €40-45, tasting menu €45; ⏲12.30-3pm & 7.30-10pm, closed Wed & dinner Sun) This refined restaurant walks the culinary high wire in Orvieto, serving inventive, artfully presented dishes, from joyful starters such as *panzanella* (a bread-based salad

ORVIETO'S WINE COUNTRY

Now renowned for its white DOC wines, Orvieto has been a wine-producing area for more than 2000 years. It was the Etruscans who first introduced viticulture to the region, recognising in its climate and volcanic soil the ideal conditions for growing vines. They carved caves into the soft tufa rock that underlies much of the surrounding countryside and left the grapes to slowly ferment. Today, wine is still stored in cool underground cellars cut into the tufa.

From the Middle Ages, Orvieto became famous in Italy and beyond for its super-sweet gold-coloured wines. Nowadays these have largely given way to drier blends, such as Orvieto DOC and Orvieto Classico.

To really immerse yourself in Orvieto's wine heritage, spend a night or two at the **Locanda Palazzone** (☎0763 39 36 14; www.locandapalazzone.com; Rocca Ripesena 67; ste from €200, apt €300-385; P 🛜 ≋), a highly respected local winery offering tastings and wine-making tours. These range from a simple three-wine tasting (€15) to tours of the winery (€25 to €45 including appetisers or a light lunch) and four-course wine-tasting dinners (€70).

Another winery worth searching out is **Decugnano dei Barbi** (☎0763 30 82 55; www.decugnanodeibarbi.com; Località Fossatello 50) 🍃, 18km east of Orvieto. You can tour its cellars – wines are stored in Etruscan tombs – and taste its minerally whites and Orvieto Classico reds (tastings €30 to €50 per person). For something more hands-on, sign up for one of its four-hour cookery classes (€95 to €150 per person).

CANADASTOCK/SHUTTERSTOCK ©

Orvieto

typical of central Italy) with vegetables and anchovies to pasta so light it almost floats off the fork. In good weather, try to get a table in the back garden. Dress for dinner and reserve ahead.

Drinking & Nightlife

Bottega Vera WINE BAR
(☎349 4300167; www.casaveraorvieto.it; Via del Duomo 36; ⏰8.30am-8.30pm Mon-Fri & Sun, to 10pm Sat; 📶) This stylish gourmet deli and wine shop has been pouring the good stuff since 1938, when it was started by grandmother of current host Cesare, who will expertly guide you through his daily selections of wine by the glass (from €3). Of Cesare's 120 wines or so, half are from Orvieto.

Information

Tourist Office (☎0763 34 17 72; Piazza Duomo 24; ⏰8.15am-1.50pm & 4-7pm Mon-Fri, 10am-6pm Sat & Sun) Helpful office opposite the *duomo*. Can supply city maps and up-to-date information on the principal sights.

Getting There & Away

Orvieto is on the Rome–Florence A1 autostrada, while the SS71 heads north to Lago Trasimeno. Your best bet for parking is the **Parcheggio Campo della Fiera** (per hour/day €1.50/12), which has a free lift up to the historic centre. There's also metered parking on Piazza Cahen.

ROAD TRIP ESSENTIALS

Italy Driving Guide

Italy's stunning natural scenery, comprehensive road network and passion for cars makes it a wonderful road-trip destination.

DRIVING LICENCE & DOCUMENTS

- All EU driving licences are recognised in Italy.
- Travellers from other countries should obtain an International Driving Permit (IDP) through their national automobile association. This should be carried with your licence; it is not a substitute for it.

When driving in Italy you are required to carry with you:

- The vehicle registration document
- Your driving licence
- Proof of third-party liability insurance

INSURANCE

- Third-party liability insurance is mandatory for all vehicles in Italy, including cars brought in from abroad.
- If driving an EU-registered vehicle, your home country insurance is sufficient. Ask your insurer for a European Accident Statement (EAS) form, which can simplify matters in the event of an accident.
- Residents of non-EU countries should contact their insurance company to see if they need a green card international insurance certificate.
- Hire agencies provide the minimum legal insurance, but you can supplement it if you choose.

HIRING A CAR

Car-hire agencies are widespread in Italy but prebooking costs less than hiring a car once you arrive in Italy. Online booking agency Rentalcars.com (www.rentalcars.com) compares the rates of numerous car-rental companies.

The following companies have pickup locations throughout Italy:

Auto Europe (www.autoeurope.it)

Avis (www.avisautonoleggio.it)

Budget (www.budgetinternational.com)

Europcar (www.europcar.it)

Hertz (www.hertz.it)

Italy by Car (www.italybycar.it)

Maggiore (www.maggiore.it)

Sixt (www.sixt.it)

Driving Fast Facts

Right or left? Drive on the right

Manual or automatic? Mostly manual

Legal driving age 18

Top speed limit 130km/h (on autostradas)

Signature car Flaming red Ferrari or Fiat 500

Driving Tips

A representative of the Automobile Club d'Italia (ACI) offers these pearls to ease your way on Italian roads:

➡ Pay particular attention to the weather. In summer it gets very hot, but, in winter, watch out for ice, snow and fog.

➡ On the extra-urban roads and autostradas, cars must have their headlights on even during the day.

➡ Watch out for signs at the autostrada toll booths – the lanes marked 'Telepass' are for cars that pay through an automatic electronic system without stopping.

➡ Watch out in the cities – big and small – for the Limited Traffic Zones (ZTL) and pay parking. There is no universal system for indicating these or their hours.

Considerations before renting

➡ Bear in mind that a car is generally more hassle than it's worth in cities, so only hire one for the time you'll be on the open road.

➡ Consider vehicle size carefully. High fuel prices, extremely narrow streets and tight parking conditions mean that smaller is often better.

➡ Road signs can be iffy in remote areas, so consider booking and paying for satnav.

Standard regulations

➡ Many agencies have a minimum rental age of 25 and a maximum of 79. You can sometimes hire if you're over 21 but supplements will apply.

➡ To rent you'll need a credit card, valid driver's licence (with IDP if necessary) and passport or photo ID. Note that some companies require that you've had your licence for at least a year.

➡ Hire cars come with the minimum legal insurance, which you can supplement by purchasing additional coverage.

➡ Check with your credit-card company to see if it offers a Collision Damage Waiver, which covers you for additional damage if you use that card to pay for the car.

Motorcycles

Agencies throughout Italy rent motorbikes, ranging from small Vespas to large touring bikes. Prices start at around €35/150 per day/week for a 50cc scooter; upwards of €80/400 per day/week for a 650cc motorcycle.

BORDER CROSSINGS

Driving into Italy is fairly straightforward – thanks to the Schengen Agreement, there are no customs checks when driving in from neighbours France, Switzerland, Austria and Slovenia. For more information see Getting There & Away on p111.

BRINGING YOUR OWN VEHICLE

➡ All foreign vehicles entering Italy should display the nationality plate of its country of registration.

➡ If you're driving a left-hand-drive UK vehicle you'll have to adjust its headlights to avoid dazzling oncoming traffic.

➡ You'll need to carry snow chains in your car if travelling in mountainous areas between 15 October and 15 April.

MAPS

We recommend you purchase a good road map for your trip. The best driving maps are produced by the Touring Club Italiano (www.touringclub.com), Italy's largest map publisher. They are available at bookstores across Italy or online at the following:

Stanfords (www.stanfords.co.uk) Excellent UK-based shop that stocks many useful maps.

Omni Resources (www.omnimap.com) US-based online retailer with an impressive selection of Italian maps.

ROAD CONDITIONS

Italy's extensive road network covers the entire peninsula and with enough patience you'll be able to get just about anywhere. Most roads are in good condition but a lack of maintenance in some areas means that you should be prepared for potholes and bumpy surfaces, particularly on smaller, secondary roads.

Traffic in and around the main cities is bad during morning and evening rush hours. Coastal roads get very busy on summer weekends. As a rule, traffic is quietest between 2pm and 4pm.

Road Categories

Autostradas Italy's toll-charging motorways. On road signs they're marked by a white 'A' and number on a green background. The main north–south artery is the A1, aka the Autostrada del Sole (the 'Motorway of the Sun'), which runs from Milan to Naples via Bologna, Florence and Rome. The main road south from Naples to Reggio di Calabria is the A3. To drive on an autostrada pick up a ticket at the entry barrier and pay (by cash or credit card) as you exit.

Strade statali (state highways) Represented on maps by 'S' or 'SS'. Vary from four-lane highways to two-lane roads. The latter can be extremely slow, especially in mountainous regions.

Strade regionali (regional highways) Like SS roads but administered by regional authorities rather than the state. Coded 'SR' or 'R'.

Strade provinciali (provincial highways) Smaller and slower roads. Coded 'SP' or 'P'.

Along with their A or SS number, some Italian roads are labelled with an E number – for example, the A4 autostrada is also shown as the E64 on maps and signs. This E number refers to the road's designation on the Europe-wide E-road network. E routes, which often cross national boundaries, are generally made up of major national roads strung together.

Limited Traffic Zones

Many Italian cities, including Rome and Florence, have designated their historic centres as Limited Traffic Zones (ZTL). These areas are off-limits to unauthorised vehicles and entry points are covered by

Road Trip Websites

AUTOMOBILE ASSOCIATIONS

Automobile Club d'Italia (www.aci.it) Has a comprehensive online guide to motoring in Italy. Provides 24-hour roadside assistance , available on a pay-per-incident system.

CONDITIONS & TRAFFIC

Autostrade (www.autostrade.it) Comprehensive site with real-time traffic info on Italy's motorways. Also lists service stations, petrol prices and toll costs.

CCISS (www.cciss.it) Italian-language site with updates on road works and real-time traffic flows.

MAPS & ROUTE PLANNING

Michelin (www.viamichelin.it) Online road-trip planner.

Tutto Città (www.tuttocitta.it) Good for detailed town and city maps.

Mappy (https://en.mappy.com) Online mapping tool.

Coins

Always try to keep some coins to hand. They come in very useful for parking meters.

street cameras. If you're caught entering one without the necessary permission you risk a fine. Being in a hire car will not exempt you from this rule.

Contact your hotel or accommodation supplier if you think you'll need to access a ZTL.

ROAD RULES

➡ Drive on the right; overtake on the left.

➡ It's obligatory to wear seat belts (front and rear), to drive with your headlights on outside built-up areas, and to carry a warning triangle and fluorescent waistcoat in case of breakdown.

➡ Wearing a helmet is compulsory on all two-wheeled vehicles.

➡ Motorbikes can enter most restricted traffic areas in Italian cities, and traffic police generally turn a blind eye to motorcycles or scooters parked on footpaths.

➡ The blood alcohol limit is 0.05%; it's zero for drivers under 21 and for those who have had their licence for less than three years.

Unless otherwise indicated, speed limits are as follows:

➡ 130km/h on autostradas

➡ 110km/h on main roads outside built-up areas

Driving Problem Buster

I can't speak Italian, will that be a problem? When at a petrol station you might have to ask the attendant for your fill-up. Ask for the amount you want, so *venti euro* for €20 or *pieno* for full. Always specify *benzina senza piombo* for unleaded petrol or *gasolio* for diesel.

What should I do if my car breaks down? Call the service number of your car-hire company. The Automobile Club d'Italia (ACI) provides 24-hour roadside assistance – call 803 116 from an Italian landline or mobile, or 800 116800 from a foreign mobile phone. Foreigners do not have to join but instead pay a per-incident fee. Note that in the event of a breakdown, a warning triangle is compulsory, as is use of an approved yellow or orange safety vest if you leave your vehicle.

What if I have an accident? For minor accidents there's no need to call the police. Fill in an accident report – Constatazione Amichevole di Incidente (CAI; Agreed Motor Accident Statement) – through your car-hire firm or insurance company.

What should I do if I get stopped by the police? The police will want to see your passport (or photo ID), licence, car registration papers and proof of insurance.

Will I need to pay tolls in advance? No. When you join an autostrada you have to pick up a ticket at the barrier. When you exit you pay based on the distance you've covered. Pay by cash or credit card.

Are the road signs easy to understand? Most signs are fairly obvious but it helps to know that town/city centres are indicated by the word *centro* and a kind of black-and-white bullseye sign; *divieto fermata* means 'no stopping'; and *tutte le direzione* means 'all directions'. See the inside back cover of this book for some of the most common road signs.

Will I be able to find ATMs along the road? Some autostrada service stations have ATMs (known as *bancomat* in Italian). Otherwise they are widely available in towns and cities.

- 90km/h on secondary roads outside built-up areas
- 50km/h in built-up areas

Road Etiquette

- Italian drivers are fast, aggressive and skilful. Lane hopping and late braking are the norm and it's not uncommon to see cars tailgating at 130km/h. Don't expect cars to slow down for you or let you out. As soon as you see a gap, go for it. Italians expect the unexpected and react swiftly, but they're not used to ditherers, so be decisive.
- Headlight flashing is common on the roads and has several meanings. If a car behind you flashes it means: 'Get out of the way' or 'Don't pull out, I'm not stopping'. But if an approaching car flashes you, it's warning you that there's a police check ahead.
- Use of the car horn is widespread. It might be a warning but it might equally be an expression of frustration at slow-moving traffic or celebration that the traffic light's just turned green.

PARKING

- Parking can be a major headache. Space is at a premium in towns and cities and Italy's traffic wardens are annoyingly efficient.
- Parking spaces outlined in blue are designated for paid parking – get a ticket from the nearest meter (coins only) or *tabaccaio* (tobacconist) and display it on your dashboard. Note that charges often don't apply overnight, typically between 8pm and 8am.
- White or yellow lines almost always indicate that residential permits are needed.

Road Distances (KM)

	Bari	Bologna	Florence	Genoa	Milan	Naples	Palermo	Perugia	Reggio di Calabria	Rome	Siena	Trento	Trieste	Turin	Venice
Bologna	681														
Florence	784	106													
Genoa	996	285	268												
Milan	899	218	324	156											
Naples	322	640	534	758	858										
Palermo	734	1415	1345	1569	1633	811									
Perugia	612	270	164	432	488	408	1219								
Reggio di Calabria	490	1171	1101	1325	1389	567	272	816							
Rome	482	408	302	526	626	232	1043	170	664						
Siena	714	176	70	296	394	464	1275	103	867	232					
Trento	892	233	339	341	218	874	1626	459	1222	641	375				
Trieste	995	308	414	336	420	948	1689	543	1445	715	484	279			
Turin	1019	338	442	174	139	932	1743	545	1307	702	460	349	551		
Venice	806	269	265	387	284	899	799	394	1296	567	335	167	165	415	
Verona	808	141	247	282	164	781	1534	377	1139	549	293	97	250	295	120

Note

Distances between Palermo and mainland towns do not take into account the ferry from Reggio di Calabria to Messina. Add an extra hour to your journey time to allow for this crossing.

FUEL

➡ Staffed filling stations (*benzinai, stazioni di servizio*) are widespread. Smaller stations tend to close between about 1pm and 3.30pm and sometimes also on Sunday afternoons.

➡ Many stations have self-service *(fai da te)* pumps that you can use 24 hours a day. To use one insert a banknote into the payment machine and press the number of the pump you want.

➡ Unleaded petrol is marked as *benzina senza piombo*; diesel as *gasolio*.

➡ Italy's petrol prices are among the highest in Europe and vary from one station to another. At the time of writing, unleaded petrol was averaging €1.46 per litre; diesel €1.29 per litre.

➡ At petrol stations, it costs slightly less to fill up yourself rather than have an assistant do it for you.

➡ Fuel costs most at austostrada service stations.

SAFETY

➡ The main safety threat to motorists is theft. Hire cars and foreign vehicles are a target for robbers and although you're unlikely to have a problem, thefts do occur.

➡ As a general rule, always lock your car and never leave anything showing, particularly valuables, and certainly not overnight. If at all possible, avoid leaving luggage in an unattended car.

➡ It's a good idea to pay extra to leave your car in supervised car parks.

RADIO

➡ RAI, Italy's state broadcaster, operates three national radio stations (Radiouno, Radiodue, Radiotre) offering news, current affairs, and classical and commercial music.

➡ Isoradio, another RAI station, provides regular news and traffic bulletins.

➡ There are also thousands of commercial radio stations, many broadcasting locally. Major ones include Radio Capital, good for modern hits; Radio Deejay, aimed at a younger audience; and Radio 24, which airs news and talk shows.

Italy Travel Guide

GETTING THERE & AWAY

AIR

The following are Italy's main international airports. Car hire is available at all these airports.

Rome Fiumicino (www.adr.it/fiumicino) Officially known as Leonardo da Vinci International Airport.

Rome Ciampino (www.adr.it/ciampino) Hub for Ryanair flights to Rome.

Milan Malpensa (www.milanomalpensa-airport.com)

Milan Linate (www.milanolinate-airport.com) Milan's second airport.

Venice Marco Polo (www.veniceairport.it)

Pisa International (www.pisa-airport.com) Main international gateway for Tuscany.

Naples International (www.aeroportodinapoli.it) Also known as Capodichino.

Catania Fontanarossa (www.aeroporto.catania.it) Sicily's busiest airport.

Bergamo Orio al Serio (www.orioaeroporto.it) Used by European low-cost carriers.

Turin Caselle (www.aeroportoditorino.it)

Bologna Guglielmo Marconi (www.bologna-airport.it)

Bari Karol Wojtyła (www.aeroportidipuglia.it)

Palermo Falcone-Borsellino (www.gesap.it)

Cagliari Elmas (www.cagliariairport.it) Main gateway for Sardinia.

CAR & MOTORCYCLE

Aside from the coastal roads linking Italy with France and Slovenia, border crossings into Italy mostly involve tunnels through the Alps (open year-round) or mountain passes (seasonally closed and requiring snow chains).

The major points of entry are the following:

Austria From Innsbruck to Bolzano via A22/E45 (Brenner Pass); Villach to Tarvisio via A23/E55.

France From Nice to Ventimiglia via A10/E80; Modane to Turin via A32/E70 (Fréjus Tunnel); Chamonix to Courmayeur via A5/E25 (Mont Blanc Tunnel).

Slovenia From Sežana to Trieste via SR58/E70.

Switzerland From Martigny to Aosta via SS27/E27 (Grand St Bernard Tunnel); Lugano to Como via A9/E35.

SEA

International car ferries sail to Italy from Albania, Croatia, France (Corsica), Greece, Malta, Montenegro, Morocco, Slovenia, Spain and Tunisia. Some routes only operate in summer, when ticket prices rise. Prices for vehicles vary according to their size. Car hire is not always available at ports, so check beforehand.

The helpful website www.directferries.co.uk allows you to search routes and compare prices between international ferry companies.

Principal operators include the following:

Adria Ferries (www.adriaferries.com) Albania to Bari (nine hours), Ancona (20 hours), Trieste (37 hours).

Anek Lines (www.anekitalia.com) Greece to Bari (eight to 18½ hours), Ancona (eight to 22 hours), Venice (25 to 32 hours).

GNV (Grandi Navi Veloci; www.gnv.it) Spain to Genoa (20 hours).

Grimaldi Lines (www.grimaldi-lines.com) Spain to Civitavecchia (20 hours), Savona (17 to 20 hours).

Jadrolinija (www.jadrolinija.hr) Croatia to Ancona (from nine hours), Bari (10 hours).

Minoan Lines (www.minoan.it) Greece to Ancona (17 to 23 hours).

Montenegro Lines (www.montenegrolines.net) Bar to Bari (10 hours).

Superfast (www.superfast.com) Greece to Bari (nine to 16 hours), Ancona (eight to 22 hours), Venice (14 to 33 hours).

TRAIN

Regular trains on two western lines connect Italy with France (one along the coast and the other from Turin into the French Alps). Trains from Milan head north into Switzerland and on towards the Benelux countries. Further east, two lines connect with Central and Eastern Europe.

Car hire is generally available at principal city stations.

Practicalities

Smoking Banned in enclosed public spaces, which includes restaurants, bars, shops and public transport.

Time Italy uses the 24-hour clock and is on Central European Time, one hour ahead of GMT/UTC.

TV The main terrestrial channels are Rai 1, 2 and 3 run by Rai (www.rai.it), Italy's state-owned national broadcaster, and Canale 5, Italia 1 and Rete 4 run by Mediaset (www.mediaset.it).

Weights & Measures Italy uses the metric system, so kilometres not miles, litres not gallons.

DIRECTORY A–Z

ACCESSIBLE TRAVEL

Italy is not an easy country for travellers with disabilities. Cobblestone streets and pavements blocked by parked cars and scooters make getting around difficult for wheelchair users. And while many buildings have lifts, they are not always wide enough for wheelchairs. Not a lot has been done to make life easier for hearing- or vision-impaired travellers either. However, awareness of accessibility issues and a culture of inclusion are steadily growing.

- The Italian National Tourist Office in your country may be able to provide advice on Italian associations for travellers with disabilities and information on what help is available.
- Airline companies will arrange assistance at airports if you notify them of your needs in advance. For help at Rome's Fiumicino or Ciampino airports contact ADR Assistance (www.adrassistance.it).
- Some taxis are equipped to carry passengers in wheelchairs; ask for a taxi for a *sedia a rotelle* (wheelchair).
- If you are driving, EU disabled parking permits are recognised in Italy, giving you the same parking rights that local drivers with disabilities have.
- If you have an obvious disability and/or appropriate ID, many museums and galleries offer free admission for yourself and a companion.

Resources include the following:

Village for All (www.villageforall.net/en) Performs on-site audits of tourist facilities in Italy and San Marino. Most of the 67 facilities are accommodation providers, ranging from camping grounds to high-class hotels.

Tourism without Barriers (www.turismosenzabarriere.it) Has a searchable database of accessible accommodation and tourist attractions in Tuscany, with a scattering of options in other regions.

Fondazione Cesare Serono (www.fondazioneserono.org/disabilita/spiagge-accessibili/spiagge-accessibili) A list (in Italian) of accessible beaches.

Accommodation Tax

- Italy's *tassa di soggiorno* (accommodation tax) sees visitors charged an extra €1 to €7 per night as a 'room occupancy tax'.
- Exactly how much you're charged depends on the type of accommodation (campground, guesthouse, hotel), a hotel's star rating, and the number of people under your booking.
- Our listings do not include the hotel tax, although it's always a good idea to confirm whether taxes are included when booking.

Download Lonely Planet's free Accessible Travel guide from http://shop.lonelyplanet.com/accessible-travel.

ACCOMMODATION

From dreamy villas to chic boutique hotels, historic hideaways and ravishing farm stays *(agriturismi)*, Italy offers accommodation to suit every taste and budget.

Seasons & Rates

- Accommodation rates fluctuate enormously from high to low season, and even from day to day depending on demand, season and booking method (online, through an agency etc).
- As a rule, peak rates apply at Easter, in summer (July and August) and over the Christmas/New Year period. But there are exceptions – in the mountains, high season means the ski season (December to late March). Also, August is high season on the coast but low season in many cities where hotels offer discounts.
- Southern Italy is generally cheaper than the north.

Reservations

- Always book ahead in peak season, even if it's only for the first night or two.
- Reserving a room is essential during key festivals and events when demand is very high.
- In the off-season, it always pays to call ahead to check that a hotel is open. Many coastal hotels close for winter, typically opening from late March or Easter to late October.
- Hotels usually require that reservations be confirmed with a credit-card number. No-shows will be docked one night's accommodation.

B&Bs

B&Bs are a burgeoning sector of the Italian accommodation market and can be found throughout the country in both urban and rural settings. Options include everything from restored farmhouses, city *palazzi* (mansions) and seaside bungalows to rooms in family houses. In some cases, a B&B can also refer to a self-contained apartment with basic breakfast provisions provided. Tariffs for a double room cover a wide range, from around €60 to €140.

Hotels & Pensioni

While the difference between an *albergo* (hotel) and a *pensione* is often minimal, a *pensione* will generally be of one- to three-star quality while an *albergo* can be awarded up to five stars. *Locande* (inns) long fell into much the same category as *pensioni*, but the term has become a trendy one in some parts and reveals little about the quality of a place. *Affittacamere* are simple rooms for rent in private houses.

All hotels are rated from one to five stars:

- One-star hotels and *pensioni* tend to be basic and often do not offer private bathrooms.
- Two-star places are similar but rooms will generally have a private bathroom.

Sleeping Price Ranges

The following price ranges refer to a double room with private bathroom (breakfast included) in high season.

€ less than €110

€€ €110–€200

€€€ more than €200

➡ Three-star hotel rooms will come with a hairdryer, minibar (or fridge), safe and air-con.

➡ Four- and five-star hotels offer facilities such as room service, laundry and dry-cleaning.

Tourist offices usually have booklets with local accommodation listings. Many hotels are also signing up with online accommodation-booking services.

Agriturismi

From rustic country houses to luxurious estates and fully functioning farms, Italian farm stays, known as *agriturismi* (singular – *agriturismo*) are hugely popular. Comfort levels, facilities and prices vary but the best will offer swimming pools and top-class accommodation. Many also operate restaurants specialising in traditional local cuisine.

For listings and further details, check the following:

Agriturismo.it (www.agriturismo.it)

Agriturismo.net (www.agriturismo.net)

Agriturismo.com (www.agriturismo.com)

Agriturismo-Italia.net (www.agriturismo-italia.net)

Other Options

Camping A popular summer option. Most campsites are big, summer-only complexes with swimming pools, restaurants and supermarkets. Many have space for RVs and offer bungalows or simple, self-contained flats. Minimum stays sometimes apply in high season. Check out www.campeggi.com and www.camping.it.

Hostels Official HI hostels and a growing contingent of independent hostels offer dorm beds and private rooms. Breakfast is usually included in rates and dinner is sometimes available for about €10 to €15. For listings and further details, see www.aighostels.com or www.hostelworld.com.

Convents & Monasteries Some convents and monasteries provide basic accommodation. Expect curfews, few frills and value for money. Useful resources include www.stpatricksamericanrome.org and www.initaly.com/agri/convents.htm.

Refuges Mountain huts *(rifugi)* with rooms sleeping anything from two to a dozen or more people. Many also offer hot meals and/or communal cooking facilities. Generally open from June to late September.

Villas Villas and *fattorie* (farmhouses) can be rented in their entirety or sometimes by the room. Many have swimming pools.

ELECTRICITY

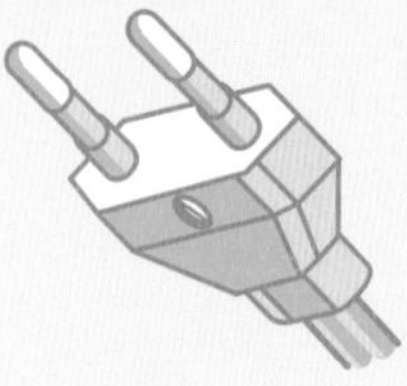

230V/50Hz

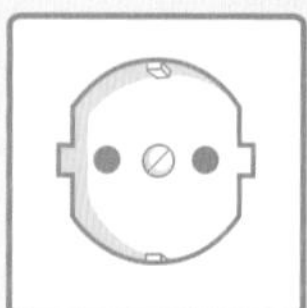

230V/50Hz

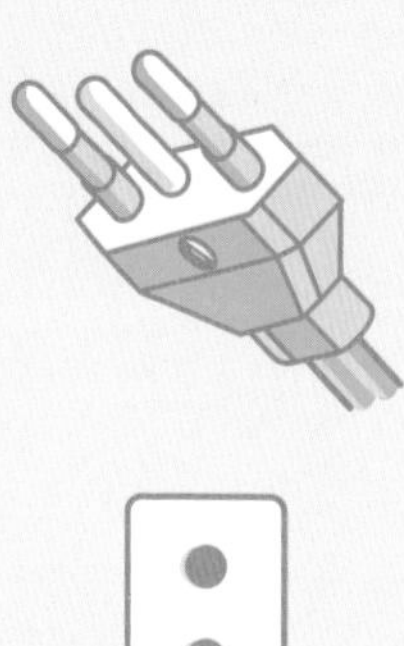

230V/50Hz

FOOD

A full Italian meal consists of an antipasto (appetiser), *primo* (first course, usually a pasta, risotto or polenta), *secondo* (second course, meat or fish) with *contorno* (vegetable side dish) or *insalata* (salad), and *dolce* (dessert) and/or fruit. When eating out it's perfectly OK to mix and match and order, say, a *primo* followed by an *insalata* or *contorno*.

Where to Eat

Italy has no shortage of eating options, and reserving a table on the day of your meal is usually fine. Top-end restaurants may need to be booked a month or more in advance, while popular eateries in tourist areas should be booked at least a few days ahead in peak season.

Ristorante (Restaurant) Formal dining, often with comprehensive wine lists and more sophisticated local or national fare.

Trattoria Informal, family-run restaurant cooking up traditional regional dishes. Generally cheap to mid-range.

Osteria Similar to a trattoria, with a focus on traditional cooking.

Enoteca Wine bars invariably double as a casual place to graze or dine, typically serving snacks such as cheese, cold meats, bruschette and *crostini* (little toasts) to accompany your tipple.

Agriturismo A farmhouse offering food made with farm-grown produce. Booking generally required.

Pizzeria Alongside pizza, many pizzerias also offer antipasti, pastas, meat and vegetable dishes. They're often only open in the evening. The best have a wood-oven *(forno a legna)*.

Bar & Cafe Italians often breakfast on a *cornetto* (Italian croissant) and cappuccino at a bar or cafe. Many places sell *panini* (bread rolls with simple fillers) at lunchtime and serve a buffet of hot and cold dishes during the early evening *aperitivo* (aperitif) hour.

Market Most towns and cities have morning produce markets where you can stock up on picnic provisions.

HEALTH

- Italy has a public health system (Servizio Sanitario Nazionale; SSN) that is legally bound to provide emergency care to everyone.
- EU nationals are entitled to reduced-cost, sometimes free, medical care with a European Health Insurance Card (EHIC), available from your home health authority.
- Non-EU citizens should take out medical insurance.
- For emergency treatment, go to the *pronto soccorso* (casualty department) of an *ospedale*

Eating Price Ranges

The following price ranges refer to a two-course meal with a glass of house wine and *coperto* (cover charge).

€ less than €25

€€ €25–€45

€€€ more than €45

Note that most eating establishments add a *coperto* of around €2 to €3. Some also include a service charge *(servizio)* of 10% to 15%.

(public hospital), though be prepared for a long wait.

➡ Pharmacists can give advice and sell over-the-counter medication for minor illnesses.

➡ Pharmacies typically open from 8.30am to 7.30pm Monday to Friday and on Saturday mornings. Outside these hours, they open on a rotational basis. When closed, a pharmacy is legally required to post a list of places open in the vicinity.

➡ In larger cities, English-speaking doctors are often available for house calls or appointments through private clinics.

➡ Italian tap water is fine to drink.

➡ No vaccinations are required for travel to Italy.

LGBT+ TRAVELLERS

➡ Homosexuality is legal in Italy and even widely accepted in the major cities. However, discretion is still wise and overt displays of affection by LGBT+ couples can attract a negative response, especially in smaller towns.

➡ There are gay venues in Rome, Milan and Bologna, and a handful in places such as Florence and Naples. Some coastal towns and resorts (such as the Tuscan town of Viareggio or Taormina in Sicily) have much more action in summer.

Resources include the following:

Arcigay (www.arcigay.it) Bologna-based national organisation for the LGBT+ community.

Gay.it (www.gay.it) Website featuring LGBT+ news, features and gossip.

Pride (www.prideonline.it) Culture, politics, travel and health with an LGBT+ focus.

Tipping Guide

Italians are not big tippers. The following is a rough guide.

Taxis Optional, but most round up to the nearest euro.

Hotels Tip porters about €5 at high-end hotels.

Restaurants Service *(servizio)* is generally included – otherwise, a euro or two is fine in pizzerias and trattorias, and 5% to 10% in smart restaurants.

Bars Not necessary, although many leave small change if drinking coffee at the bar, usually €0.10 or €0.20.

INTERNET ACCESS

➡ Free wi-fi is widely available in hotels, hostels, B&Bs and *agriturismi* (farm stays), though signal quality varies. Some places also provide laptops/computers.

➡ Many bars and cafes offer free wi-fi.

➡ Numerous Italian cities and towns offer public wi-fi hotspots, including Rome, Milan, Bologna, Florence and Venice. To use them, you'll need to register online using a credit card or an Italian mobile number.

➡ A free smartphone app, wifi.italia.it, allows you to connect to participating networks through a single login. Released in summer 2017, it gets mixed reports.

MONEY

Italy uses the euro. Euro notes come in denominations of €500, €200, €100, €50, €20, €10 and €5; coins come in denominations of €2 and €1, and 50, 20, 10, five, two and one cents.

For the latest exchange rates, check out www.xe.com.

Admission Prices

➡ State museums and sites offer free admission to under-18s and discounted entry to 18- to 25-year-olds.

➡ You'll need photo ID to claim reduced entry.

➡ State-run museums are free on the first Sunday of the month between October and March.

ATMs & Credit Cards

➡ ATMs (known as *bancomat*) are widely available throughout Italy and most will accept cards tied into the Visa, MasterCard, Cirrus and Maestro systems.

➡ Credit cards such as Visa, MasterCard, Eurocard, Cirrus and Eurocheques are widely accepted. Amex is also recognised, though less common.

➡ Virtually all midrange and top-end hotels accept credit cards, as do most restaurants and large shops. Some cheaper *pensioni* (pensions), trattorias and pizzerias only accept cash. Don't rely on credit cards at smaller museums or galleries.

➡ Always inform your bank of your travel plans to avoid your card being blocked for payments made in unusual locations.

➡ Check any charges with your bank. Most banks charge a foreign exchange fee as well as a transaction charge of around 1% to 3%.

➡ If your card is lost, stolen or swallowed by an ATM, call to have it blocked:

Amex ☎06 7290 0347

Diners Club ☎800 393939

MasterCard ☎800 870866

Visa ☎800 819014

Moneychangers

➡ You can change money at a *cambio* (exchange office) or post office. Some banks might change money, though many now only do this for account holders. Post offices and banks offer the best rates; exchange offices keep longer hours, but watch for high commissions and inferior rates.

➡ Take your passport or photo ID when exchanging money.

OPENING HOURS

Opening hours vary throughout the year. We've provided high-season hours, which are generally in use over summer. Summer refers to the period between April and September (or October); winter is October (or November) to March.

Banks 8.30am–1.30pm and 2.45pm–4.30pm Monday to Friday

Bars & cafes 7.30am–8pm, sometimes to 1am or 2am

Clubs 10pm–4am or 5am

Restaurants noon–3pm and 7.30pm–11pm (later in summer)

Shops 9am–1pm and 3.30pm–7.30pm (or 4pm to 8pm) Monday to Saturday. In main cities some shops stay open at lunchtime and on Sunday mornings. Some shops close Monday mornings.

Italian Wine Classifications

Italian wines are classified according to strict quality-control standards and carry one of four denominations:

DOCG (*Denominazione di Origine Controllata e Garantita*) Italy's best wines; made in specific areas according to stringent production rules.

DOC (*Denominazione di Origine Controllata*) Quality wines produced in defined regional areas.

IGT (*Indicazione di Geografica Tipica*) Wines typical of a certain region.

Vino da Tavola Wines for everyday drinking; often served as house wine in trattorias.

PUBLIC HOLIDAYS

Most Italians take their annual holiday in August. Many businesses and shops close for at least part of the month, particularly around Ferragosto (Feast of the Assumption) on 15 August.

Individual towns have public holidays to celebrate the feasts of their patron saints. National public holidays include the following:

Capodanno (New Year's Day) 1 January

Epifania (Epiphany) 6 January

Pasquetta (Easter Monday) March/April

Giorno della Liberazione (Liberation Day) 25 April

Festa del Lavoro (Labour Day) 1 May

Festa della Repubblica (Republic Day) 2 June

Ferragosto (Feast of the Assumption) 15 August

Festa di Ognisanti (All Saints' Day) 1 November

Festa dell'Immacolata Concezione (Feast of the Immaculate Conception) 8 December

Natale (Christmas Day) 25 December

Festa di Santo Stefano (Boxing Day) 26 December

Important Numbers

Italy country code (☎39)

International access code (☎00)

Police (☎112, 113)

Ambulance (☎118)

Fire (☎115)

Roadside assistance (☎803 116 from an Italian landline or mobile phone; ☎800 116800 from a foreign mobile phone)

SAFE TRAVEL

Italy is a safe country but petty theft can be a problem. There's no need for paranoia but be aware that thieves and pickpockets operate in touristy areas, so watch out when exploring the sights in Rome, Florence, Venice and Naples.

Cars, particularly those with foreign number plates or rental-company stickers, provide rich pickings for thieves.

In case of theft or loss, report the incident to the police within 24 hours and ask for a statement.

Some tips:

- Wear your bag/camera strap across your body and away from the road – thieves on scooters can swipe a bag and be gone in seconds.
- Never drape your bag over an empty chair at a street-side cafe or put it where you can't see it. Also, never leave valuables in coat pockets in restaurants or other places with communal coat hooks.
- Always check your change to see you haven't been short changed.

TELEPHONE

Domestic Calls

- Italian area codes begin with 0 and consist of up to four digits. They are an integral part of all phone numbers and must be dialled even when calling locally.
- Mobile-phone numbers begin with a three-digit prefix starting with a 3.
- Toll-free numbers are known as *numeri verdi* and usually start with 800.
- Some six-digit national rate numbers are also in use (such as those for Alitalia and Trenitalia).

International Calls

- To call Italy from abroad, dial your country's international access code, then Italy's country code (39) followed by the area code of the location you want (including the first zero) and the rest of the number.
- To call abroad from Italy dial 00, then the country code, followed by the full number.
- Avoid making international calls from hotels, as rates are high.
- The cheapest way to call is to use an app such as Skype or Viber, connecting through the wi-fi at your hotel/B&B etc.

Mobile Phones

- Italian mobile phones operate on the GSM 900/1800 network, which is compatible with the rest of Europe and Australia but not always with the North American GSM or CDMA systems – check with your service provider.
- The cheapest way of using your mobile is to buy a prepaid *(prepagato)* Italian SIM card. TIM (Telecom Italia Mobile; www.tim.it), Wind (www.wind.it), Vodafone (www.vodafone.it) and Tre (www.tre.it) all offer SIM cards and have retail outlets across the country. You can then top up as you go, either online or at one of your provider's shops.
- Note that by Italian law all SIM cards must be registered in Italy, so make sure you have your passport or ID card when you buy one.

TOILETS

Besides in museums, galleries, train stations and autostrada service stations, there are few public toilets in Italy. If you're caught short, the best thing to do is to nip into a cafe or bar. The polite thing to do is to order something at the bar.

You may need to pay to use some public toilets (usually €0.50 to €1.50).

TOURIST INFORMATION

- Italy's national tourist board, ENIT – Agenzia Nazionale del Turismo – has offices across the world. Its website, www.italia.it, provides both practical information and inspirational travel ideas.
- Most cities and towns in Italy have a tourist office that can provide maps, lists of local accommodation, and information on sights in the area.
- In larger towns and major tourist areas, English is generally spoken, along with other languages, depending on the region (for example, German in Alto Adige, French in Valle d'Aosta).
- Most tourist offices will respond to written or telephone requests for information.
- Office hours vary: in major tourist destinations, offices generally open daily, especially in the summer high season. In smaller centres, they generally observe regular office hours and open Monday through to Friday, perhaps also on Saturday mornings.
- Affiliated information booths (at train stations and airports, for example) may keep slightly different hours.
- Tourist offices in Italy go under a variety of names, depending on who they're administered by (the local municipality, province, or region), but most perform similar functions. On the ground, look for signs to the *Ufficio Turistico*.

Regional Tourist Authorities

Regional offices are generally more concerned with marketing and promotion than offering a public information service. However, they have useful websites.

Abruzzo (www.abruzzoturismo.it)

Basilicata (www.basilicataturistica.it)

Calabria (www.turiscalabria.it)

Campania (www.incampania.com)

Emilia-Romagna (www.emiliaromagna turismo.it)

Friuli Venezia Giulia (www.turismo.fvg.it)

Lazio (www.visitlazio.com)

Le Marche (www.turismo.marche.it)

Liguria (www.lamialiguria.it)

Lombardy (www.in-lombardia.it)

Molise (www.visitmolise.eu)

Piedmont (www.piemonteitalia.eu)

Puglia (www.viaggiareinpuglia.it)

Sardinia (www.sardegnaturismo.it)

Sicily (www.visitsicily.info)

Trentino-Alto Adige (www.visittrentino.it)

Tuscany (www.visittuscany.com)

Umbria (www.umbriatourism.it)

Valle d'Aosta (www.lovevda.it)

Veneto (www.veneto.eu)

VISAS

- Italy is one of the 26 European countries making up the Schengen area. There are no customs controls when travelling between Schengen countries, so the visa rules that apply to Italy apply to all Schengen countries.
- EU citizens do not need a visa to enter Italy.
- Nationals of some other countries, including Australia, Canada, Israel, Japan, New Zealand, Switzerland and the USA, do not need a visa for stays of up to 90 days.
- Nationals of other countries will need a Schengen tourist visa – to check requirements see www.schengenvisainfo.com/tourist-schengen-visa.
- All non-EU and non-Schengen nationals entering Italy for more than 90 days or for any reason other than tourism (such as study or work) may need a specific visa. Check http://vistoperitalia.esteri.it for details.
- Ensure your passport is valid for at least six months beyond your departure date from Italy.

Language

Italian sounds can all be found in English. If you read our coloured pronunciation guides as if they were English, you'll be understood. Note that ai is pronounced as in 'aisle', ay as in 'say', ow as in 'how', dz as the 'ds' in 'lids', and that r is strong and rolled. If the consonant is written as a double letter, it's pronounced a little stronger, eg *sonno* son·no (sleep) versus *sono* so·no (I am). The stressed syllables are indicated with italics.

BASICS

Hello.	*Buongiorno.*	bwon·jor·no
Goodbye.	*Arrivederci.*	a·ree·ve·der·chee
Yes./No.	*Sì./No.*	see/no
Excuse me.	*Mi scusi.*	mee skoo·zee
Sorry.	*Mi dispiace.*	mee dees·pya·che
Please.	*Per favore.*	per fa·vo·re
Thank you.	*Grazie.*	gra·tsye

You're welcome.
Prego. pre·go

Do you speak English?
Parli inglese? par·lee een·gle·ze

I don't understand.
Non capisco. non ka·pee·sko

How much is this?
Quanto costa questo? kwan·to kos·ta kwe·sto

ACCOMMODATION

Do you have a room?
Avete una camera? a·ve·te oo·na ka·me·ra

How much is it per night/person?
Quanto costa per una notte/persona? kwan·to kos·ta per oo·na no·te/per·so·na

DIRECTIONS

Where's ...?
Dov'è ...? do·ve ...

Can you show me (on the map)?
Può mostrarmi (sulla pianta)? pwo mos·trar·mee (soo·la pyan·ta)

EATING & DRINKING

What would you recommend?
Cosa mi consiglia? ko·za mee kon·see·lya

I'd like ..., please.
Vorrei ..., per favore. vo·ray ... per fa·vo·re

I don't eat (meat).
Non mangio (carne). non man·jo (kar·ne)

Please bring the bill.
Mi porta il conto, per favore? mee por·ta eel kon·to per fa·vo·re

EMERGENCIES

Help!
Aiuto! a·yoo·to

I'm lost.
Mi sono perso/a. (m/f) mee so·no per·so/a

I'm ill.
Mi sento male. mee sen·to ma·le

Call the police!
Chiami la polizia! kya·mee la po·lee·tsee·a

Call a doctor!
Chiami un medico! kya·mee oon me·dee·ko

Want More?

For in-depth language information and handy phrases, check out Lonely Planet's *Italian Phrasebook*. You'll find it at **shop.lonelyplanet.com**, or you can buy Lonely Planet's iPhone phrasebooks at the Apple App Store.

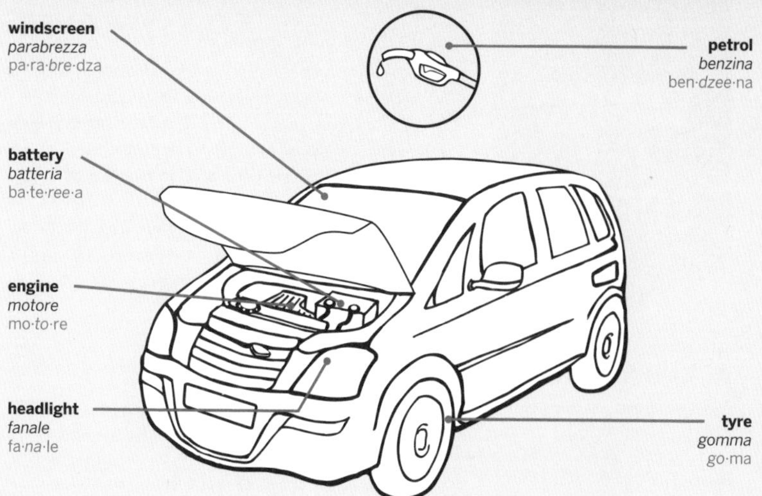

ON THE ROAD

I'd like to hire a/an ... *Vorrei noleggiare ...* vo·*ray* no·le·*ja*·re ...

4WD	*un fuoristrada*	oon fwo·ree·*stra*·da
automatic/ manual	*una macchina automatica/ manuale*	*oo*·na *ma*·kee·na ow·to·*ma*·tee·ka/ ma·noo·*a*·le
motorbike	*una moto*	*oo*·na *mo*·to

How much is it ...? *Quanto costa ...?* *kwan*·to *kos*·ta ...

daily	*al giorno*	al *jor*·no
weekly	*alla settimana*	*a*·la se·tee·*ma*·na

Does that include insurance?
E' compresa l'assicurazione? e kom·*pre*·sa la·see·koo·ra·*tsyo*·ne

Does that include mileage?
E' compreso il chilometraggio? e kom·*pre*·so eel kee·lo·me·*tra*·jo

What's the city/country speed limit?
Qual'è il limite di velocità in città/campagna? kwa·le eel *lee*·mee·te dee ve·lo·chee·*ta* een chee·*ta*/kam·*pa*·nya

Is this the road to (Venice)?
Questa strada porta a (Venezia)? *kwe*·sta *stra*·da *por*·ta a (ve·*ne*·tsya)

(How long) Can I park here?
(Per quanto tempo) Posso parcheggiare qui? (per *kwan*·to *tem*·po) *po*·so par·ke·*ja*·re kwee

Please fill it up.
Il pieno, per favore. eel *pye*·no per fa·*vo*·re

Where's a service station?
Dov'è una stazione di servizio? do·*ve oo*·na sta·*tsyo*·ne dee ser·*vee*·tsyo

I'd like (30) litres.
Vorrei (trenta) litri. vo·*ray* (*tren*·ta) *lee*·tree

Please check the oil/water.
Può controllare l'olio/ l'acqua, per favore? pwo kon·tro·*la*·re *lo*·lyo/ *la*·kwa per fa·*vo*·re

I need a mechanic.
Ho bisogno di un meccanico. o bee·*zo*·nyo dee oon me·*ka*·nee·ko

The car/motorbike has broken down.
La macchina/moto si è guastata. la *ma*·kee·na/*mo*·to see e gwas·*ta*·ta

I had an accident.
Ho avuto un incidente. o a·*voo*·to oon een·chee·*den*·te

Signs

Alt	Stop
Dare la Precedenza	Give Way
Deviazione	Detour
Divieto di Accesso	No Entry
Entrata	Entrance
Pedaggio	Toll
Senso Unico	One Way
Uscita	Exit

SEND US YOUR FEEDBACK

We love to hear from travellers – your comments help make our books better. We read every word, and we guarantee that your feedback goes straight to the authors. Visit **lonelyplanet.com/contact** to submit your updates and suggestions.

Note: We may edit, reproduce and incorporate your comments in Lonely Planet products such as guidebooks, websites and digital products, so let us know if you don't want your comments reproduced or your name acknowledged. For a copy of our privacy policy visit lonelyplanet.com/privacy.

ACKNOWLEDGMENTS

Climate map data adapted from Peel MC, Finlayson BL & McMahon TA (2007) 'Updated World Map of the Köppen-Geiger Climate Classification', *Hydrology and Earth System Sciences*, 11, 1633-44.

Cover photographs: Front: Val d'Orcia, Marco Bottigelli/AWL Images; Back: Duomo, Florence, Jan Christopher Becke/AWL Images

THIS BOOK

This 2nd edition of *Tuscany Road Trips* was researched and written by Duncan Garwood, Virginia Maxwell and Nicola Williams. The previous edition was written by Duncan Garwood, Paula Hardy, Robert Landon and Nicola Williams. This guidebook was produced by the following:

Destination Editor Anna Tyler

Senior Product Editor Elizabeth Jones

Product Editor Kate James

Senior Cartographer Anthony Phelan

Book Designer Katherine Marsh

Assisting Editors Charlotte Orr, Gabrielle Stefanos

Cover Researcher Meri Blazevski

Thanks to Imogen Bannister, Sasha Baskett, Hannah Cartmel, Catherine Naghten, Kirsten Rawlings

OUR STORY

A beat-up old car, a few dollars in the pocket and a sense of adventure. In 1972 that's all Tony and Maureen Wheeler needed for the trip of a lifetime – across Europe and Asia overland to Australia. It took several months, and at the end – broke but inspired – they sat at their kitchen table writing and stapling together their first travel guide, *Across Asia on the Cheap*. Within a week they'd sold 1500 copies. Lonely Planet was born.

Today, Lonely Planet has offices in Franklin, London, Melbourne, Oakland, Dublin, Beijing and Delhi, with more than 600 staff and writers. We share Tony's belief that 'a great guidebook should do three things: inform, educate and amuse'.

INDEX

SORINA CHIRITA

LONELY PLANET IN THE WILD

Send your 'Lonely Planet in the Wild' photos to social@lonelyplanet.com
We share the best on our Facebook page every week!

OUR WRITERS

DUNCAN GARWOOD
From facing fast bowlers in Barbados to sidestepping hungry pigs in Goa, Duncan's travels have thrown up many unique experiences. These days he largely dedicates himself to the Mediterranean and Italy, his adopted homeland where he's been living since 1997. He's worked on around 50 Lonely Planet titles, including guidebooks to Italy, Rome, Sardinia, Sicily, Spain and Portugal, as well as books on world food and epic drives. He's also written on Italy for newspapers, websites and magazines.

VIRGINIA MAXWELL
Although based in Australia, Virginia spends at least half of her year updating Lonely Planet destination coverage across the globe. The Mediterranean is her major area of interest – she has covered Spain, Italy, Turkey, Syria, Lebanon, Israel, Egypt, Morocco and Tunisia – but she also covers Finland, Bali, Armenia, the Netherlands, the US and Australia for Lonely Planet products. Follow her @maxwellvirginia on Instagram and Twitter.

NICOLA WILLIAMS
Border hopping is way of life for British writer, runner, foodie, art aficionado and mum-of-three Nicola Williams who has lived in a French village on the southern side of Lake Geneva for more than a decade. Nicola has authored more than 50 guidebooks on Paris, Provence, Rome, Tuscany, France, Italy and Switzerland for Lonely Planet and covers France as a destination expert for the *Telegraph*. She also writes for the *Independent*, *Guardian*, lonelyplanet.com, *Lonely Planet Magazine*, *French Magazine*, *Cool Camping France* and others. Catch her on the road on Twitter and Instagram @tripalong.

Published by Lonely Planet Global Limited
CRN 554153
2nd edition – Jun 2020
ISBN 978 1 78657 567 8
© Lonely Planet 2020 Photographs © as indicated 2020
10 9 8 7 6 5 4 3 2 1
Printed in China

Although the authors and Lonely Planet have taken all reasonable care in preparing this book, we make no warranty about the accuracy or completeness of its content and, to the maximum extent permitted, disclaim all liability arising from its use.

All rights reserved. No part of this publication may be copied, stored in a retrieval system, or transmitted in any form by any means, electronic, mechanical, recording or otherwise, except brief extracts for the purpose of review, and no part of this publication may be sold or hired, without the written permission of the publisher. Lonely Planet and the Lonely Planet logo are trademarks of Lonely Planet and are registered in the US Patent and Trademark Office and in other countries. Lonely Planet does not allow its name or logo to be appropriated by commercial establishments, such as retailers, restaurants or hotels. Please let us know of any misuses: lonelyplanet.com/ip.